Feeding the Flock

A Collection of Recipes by
1st Congregational Church of Covert
P.O. Box 86 73893 Lake Street
Covert, MI 49043

Printed in the U.S.A. by

P.O. Box 2110 • Kearney, NE 68848
800-445-6621 • www.morriscookbooks.com

66230-ck   1

Covert Congregational Church

The Covert Congregational Sunday School was organized in 1868[26] under the leadership of D.B. Allen, school superintendent. Classes were held in a barn that was being used as a temporary school building. This group of people moved ahead and organized as an official Congregational Church September 27, 1870 with these twenty charter members:

Josiah Packard
Mrs. Elizabeth Naomi
  Packard
Miss Perlia Packard
Milan Packard
William Packard
Mrs. Mary F. Packard
Alfred Smith Packard
Miss Permilia Packard
Miss Margaret Smith
Edward Areil Rood
Mrs. Flora Mary Rood
Edgar Shaw
Mrs. Barbara Shaw
William Frederick
  Trafford
Mrs. Martha Electa
  Trafford
Gordon Sinclair
Thaddeus Rood
Mrs. Martha Rood
David Brainard Allen
Mrs. Flora Altheda Allen

These charter members were all in some way connected with the lumbering industry.

The organization of the church took place in a new barn, fitted up for a school building and for religious meetings. They were held in the barn until the new school was built in 1870. They soon outgrew these quarters and used Packard's Hall. For over six and half years, March

16, 1873 until November 2, 1879, services were held in this hall. August M. Rice, a student of the Chicago Theological Seminary, preached during the summer months, coming from Chicago by boat to South Haven, then riding by stagecoach to Covert.

In 1871, William Packard deeded the Congregational Church two lots, 17 and 18 in Covert village, to build a church and parsonage. The parsonage was built in 1873 on lot 18, and five years later, in 1878, the church was constructed on lot 17.

The first resident pastor was Rev. Frederick Bush, who moved into the completed parsonage that cost $1500.00

When Rev. Levi Spelman began his services in 1879, the church building was completed at a cost of $4,000.00, and dedicated free of debt November 5, 1879.

The bell, which was called Covertites to worship for over a hundred years, was a gift of "Uncle" William Packard on the thirteenth anniversary of the church.

The present church building and parsonage are essentially the same today. The parsonage has been used for needed Sunday School rooms for the last twenty years. The pastors during this time have lived in other places. A much needed kitchen and restrooms have been added. The church was built with the best lumber from this area, and much loving care from its' members. The Lord has always provided for the needed improvements.

There have been twenty eight pastors during the one hundred and six years of Christian ministry. The present pastor, Rev. Murlin Hansel, has been minister since 1966, and the radio broadcast, heard every Sunday morning for years, is a testimony of God's work in this present day. The Sunday School sends out a bus every Sunday morning to pick up students, much as "Uncle" William Packard picked them up many years ago by bobsled. Ray Pumfrey was the bus driver for over twenty one years. Many people have been faithful in performing services needed at a particular point in time.

Credit due to "Pearl Sarno."

Pastors of the First Congregational Church

1. Frederick Willard Bush.........................January 1, 1873-April 1, 1877
2. Ezra Judson Alden.....................................April 1, 1877-April 1, 1879
3. Levi Parsons Spelman....................August 17, 1879-August 2, 1885
4. John Jefferies...........................November 8, 1885-August 13, 1893
5. Edward G. Palmer..............................May 1, 1894-January 15, 1896
6. Elmer D. Bostwick.............................April 19, 1896-August 8, 1897
7. John P. Barrett...........................November 14, 1897-August 1, 1900
8. Luther Kendall Long..............September 26, 1900-August 13, 1905
9. Theodore C. Williams.............November 1, 1905-November 1, 1907
10. Henry Martin Lyman............................January 1, 1908-July 2, 1910
11. R. Eugene Griggs........................January 8, 1911-January 18, 1912
12. Fred Harrison...................................May 19, 1912-March 7, 1915
13. Harry B. Gebhart..........................September 1, 1916-August, 1917
14. Delivan B. Reed.....................................April 7, 1918-June 25, 1925
15. Rudolph Roth...........................August 15, 1926-November 27, 1927
16. Albert Dave.........................February 26, 1928-November 30, 1930
17. Russell H. McConnell..............December 3, 1931-February 1, 1934
18. Wm. E. Goltz.....................................April 19, 1934-March 28, 1948
19. George Lomas..July, 1948-December, 1948
20. Thomas Groome, *Student Minister*...................June, 1949-Sept., 1949
21. James Van Dyke, *Student Minister*......................May, 1950-May, 1951
22. Paul Tanis, *Student Minister*....................May, 1951-September, 1951
23. James Van Dyke, *Student Minister*..................Sept., 1951-May, 1952
24. Theodore Hard...June, 1952-June, 1953
25. Alfred Allard..June, 1953-1955
26. Wilmer McNair, *Student Minister*............June, 1955-September, 1955
27. Howard Nagle, *Layman*...1955-June, 1962
28. Adolph Marks...June, 1963-November, 1965
29. Murlin Hansel...February, 1966-
30. Steve Churchill
31. Rev. Buist
32. Duane Jones

Women's Church Club

The Ladies Aid Society was first called Ladies Social and Benevolent Society and was organized in 1884. Today it is called the Women's Church Club. Regardless of the name, their work has been one of activity and helping. The aim of the Church Club was[26] "to help with the Church expenses, aid in all social activities of the Church and in any community work." Early they studied, prepared articles and gave money to many mission projects. Sometimes, as they met together, they worked for[27] the lady where the meeting was held. They worked and saved to buy cushions for the church pews, which were ordered from Farwells of Chicago at a cost of $174.57. The cushions were placed in the church October 1, 1886. The secretary, S.E. Shaw records the next meeting as being "a pleasant afternoon in conversation about the cushions." These were later to be recovered in 1962 by Mildred Dyer at a cost of $504.50 paid for by the Church.

One day, they met at Mrs. Ballou's where they quilted and stayed for supper. At another meeting[28] they had a few short stories and articles read and the secretary, Mrs. L. Carpenter, adds "our general talk was too much like gossip." And again, after quilting for eight consecutive meetings for Mrs. Rood, the record says, "received from Mrs. David Rood $1.50 for quilting." It was recorded about another meeting "met at Mrs. Carpenter's, eleven present, had a pleasant time, made a pair of pants for Harry Turner." Other early events that are recorded by the ladies as having participated in are: Fourth of July celebrations, lawn socials, box socials, fairs, teas, suppers, pumpkin pie socials and quilting bees.

In 1887, in trying to decide how to spend their money, they voted to invite a temperance lecturer to speak. A Reverend from Kalamazoo was chosen.

Regularly, they helped with the minister's salary, often painting the church and improving the interior. In 1893, they papered the church at a cost of $145.00. Coal bills, hymnal repairs and cleaning the church were all part of their yearly plans.

At the annual meetings of 1905, 1906, 1907 and 1918, the ladies had presented to the Church Board, each year, plans to have a dining room added on the east side of the church. These plans were approved but never materialized at that time probably because of [29]"passing through 1907, a year of orchard disaster and financial panic," This, no doubt, was the severe freeze of 1907, that destroyed many orchards completely.

They have continued to quietly serve, in many ways, doing the things that needed to be done in their specific time: A gift for the pastor, flowers for the altar, painting, papering, making choir robes, helping families with food when death came, sharing recipes in a cookbook, sending gifts to missionaries, flowers and cards to shut-ins and the sick, and providing the church kitchen with equipment. Church suppers or any event that needed food, found the Women's Church Club on hand to cook and clean up.

One of many examples of their work, found recorded in their annual report of 1969 says, "a package of bandages for lepers, old eye glasses and a collection of used postage stamps for overseas shipment was sent."

Credit due to "Pearl Sarno."

Grandma's Apron

"Ruth, what would you like for Christmas?" I asked a resident at a nursing home.

"An apron," she answered quickly.

"It keeps my dress clean and washes easy."

An apron? Of all "suggested gifts"

I'd seen in magazines or newspapers there was no mention of an apron.

My Grandma Buchholz would have liked an apron. I remember how she used hers to grab a hot pot handle, to gather eggs; to carry chips from the woodpile, green beans from the garden and sprigs of sweet-smelling lilacs; she used it to shoo flies; to wipe a tear; to cover her head in a rain, and to hold the little chicks gathered up quickly when a storm struck. She used it to hold hot jars while screwing on lids and to hold a hot poker while stirring the fire.

And when a visitor was seen coming through the gate she whisked it off, dusting the table with it as she went to greet the visitor in her fresh clean dress.

Always at Christmas, when all of her grandchildren arrived, she brought forth from the apron a tan wooden pencil with pointed eraser and a handkerchief for each of us. But I never gave Grandma anything. There was a gift from the family, but nothing special from me to her, such as my grandchildren give me. How Grandmother would have enjoyed a new apron! An arm's length of pretty material hemmed and gathered at the waist with band and ties. Such an easy thing to do. I wonder why I didn't think of it. Often I wonder why I didn't think of lots of things to do for people. All about us are easy things to do to make someone happier. Take a book to a shut-in or do some shopping for her; invite a lonely friend to lunch; take an older person for a ride; send a taped conversation to a friend far away; visit a prisoner. Do one special thing, every day!

Author Unknown

Table of Contents

Soups
&
Salads

*But I am like an olive tree flourishing
in the house of God; I trust in God's
unfailing love for ever and ever.*

~ Psalm 52:8

Helpful Hints

- Fresh lemon juice will remove onion scent from hands.

- To save money, pour all leftover vegetables and water in which they are cooked into a freezer container. When full, add tomato juice and seasoning to create a "free" soup.

- Instant potatoes are a good stew thickener.

- Three large stalks of celery, chopped and added to about two cups of beans (navy, brown, pinto, etc.), will make them easier to digest.

- When cooking vegetables that grow above ground, the rule of thumb is to boil them without a cover.

- A lump of sugar added to water when cooking greens helps vegetables retain their fresh color.

- Never soak vegetables after slicing; they will lose much of their nutritional value.

- Fresh vegetables require little seasoning or cooking. If the vegetable is old, dress it up with sauces or seasoning.

- To cut down on odors when cooking cabbage, cauliflower, etc..., add a little vinegar to the cooking water.

- To avoid tears when cutting onions, try cutting them under cold running water or briefly placing them in the freezer before cutting.

- Perk up soggy lettuce by soaking it in a mixture of lemon juice and cold water.

- Vinegar can remove spots caused by tomatoes. Soak the spot with vinegar and wash as usual.

- Egg shells can be easily removed from hard-boiled eggs if they are quickly rinsed in cold water after they are boiled. Also, add a drop of food coloring to help tell the cooked eggs apart from the raw ones in your refrigerator.

- Keep bean sprouts and jicama fresh and crisp up to five days by submerging them in a container of water, then refrigerating them.

- Your fruit salads will look perfect when you use an egg slicer to make perfect slices of strawberries, kiwis, or bananas.

SOUPS & SALADS

CAULIFLOWER CHEESE SOUP

Pauline Hoadley

1 lg. head cauliflower
2 T. onion, minced
2 T. butter, melted
2 T. flour
½ tsp. salt
¼ tsp. pepper

1 can beef or chicken broth
3 c. milk
2 c. grated American or cheddar
  cheese
¼ c. parsley, opt.

Break cauliflower into small pieces. Cook covered in salt water until tender; drain. Meanwhile sauce onion in butter until tender. Blend in flour, salt and pepper. Gradually stir in broth and milk. Cook over medium heat, stirring constantly, until mixture reaches boiling point. Add cheese and stir until it melts. Add cauliflower and parsley. Heat to serving temperature. Makes 2 quarts.

CHUNKY POTATO SOUP

Pauline Hoadley

4 med. potatoes, about 2 lbs.,
  peeled & cubed
¾ c. chopped onion
1 sm. carrot, chopped
¼ c. chopped celery
1½ c. chicken broth
3 T. butter, cubed

3 T. all-purpose flour
2½ c. milk
1 T. minced fresh parsley
¾ tsp. salt
½ tsp. pepper
1 c. (4 oz.) shredded Swiss
  cheese

In a large saucepan, combine the potatoes, onion, carrot, celery and broth. Bring to a boil. Reduce heat; cover and simmer for 12-15 minutes or until vegetable are tender; lightly mash. Meanwhile, in a small saucepan, melt butter; stir in flour until smooth. Gradually stir in milk. Bring to a boil; cook and stir for 2 minutes or until thickened. Stir into potato mixture. Cook and stir until thickened and bubbly. Add parsley, salt and pepper. Remove from the heat; stir in cheese until melted. Yields: 7 servings.

HEARTY POTATO SOUP

Pauline Hoadley

6 med. potatoes, peeled & diced
2 carrots, shredded
6 celery stalks, diced
2 qt. water
1 onion, chopped
6 T. butter or margarine
6 T. all-purpose flour

1 tsp. salt (go easy on salt)
½ tsp. pepper
1½ c. whole milk or ¾ c. whole
  milk & ¾ c. half & half
2 chicken flavored bouillon
  cubes

In a large skillet, cook potatoes, carrots and celery in water with bouillon cubes until tender. Sauté onions in butter until soft. Stir in flour, salt and pepper, gradually adding milk, stirring constantly until desired consistency. Yields: 2½ quarts. Makes 8-10 servings. If you desire a smoother soup, put potatoes, carrots and celery through the blender before adding remaining ingredients.

VEGETABLE CHILI

Ruth Magner

1 lb. ground turkey
1 med. onion, diced
1 red pepper, diced
1½ c. carrots, slivered
2 c. cabbage, cut up

2 (14½-oz.) cans diced tomatoes
2 T. chili powder
Salt, pepper
Dash Italian seasoning
1 can chili beans

Brown meat in canola oil, add vegetables; simmer 40 minutes. Add beans.

ASPARAGUS POTATO SOUP

Londa Wines

2 c. diced potatoes
½ lb. fresh asparagus, chopped
½ c. chopped onions
2 celery ribs, chopped
1 T. chicken bouillon granules
4 c. water
¼ c. butter or margarine
½ c. all-purpose flour

1 c. whipping cream
½ c. milk
½ tsp. salt
Dash pepper
12 bacon strips, cooked &
  crumbled
¾ c. shredded cheddar cheese

In a large saucepan or soup kettle, combine potatoes, asparagus, onion, celery, bouillon and water. Bring to boil, reduce heat; cover and simmer for 15 minutes or until vegetables are tender. Stir in butter. In a bowl combine flour, milk, cream, salt, pepper until smooth; add to the vegetable mixture. Bring to a boil, cook and stir for 2 minutes or until thick. Garnish with bacon and cheese.

66230-05

WILD RICE SOUP

Bob Wines

2 to 3 strips bacon, cut up	4 to 4½ c. chicken stock
⅔ c. wild rice, rinsed	1 to 1½ c. heavy cream
½ c. onion, chopped	1 T. butter, softened
½ c. carrots, diced	1 T. all-purpose flour
½ c. celery, cut up	Salt & pepper

Fry bacon, drain and reserve 2 tablespoons fat. Sauté rice, onion, carrots and celery in bacon fat for 5 minutes. Return bacon to kettle. Stir in 4 cups of the stock. Heat, stirring constantly to boiling; reduce heat. Simmer covered, stirring occasionally until rice is tender, about 40 minutes. Stir in 1 cup of the cream. Mix the butter and flour, whisk into soup. Cook, stirring constantly until the soup thickens and bubbles, about 1 minute. Stir in the remaining ½ cup of stock and ½ cup cream, if a thinner soup is desired. Season to taste. Makes about 8 cups.

DUMP SOUP
(Originally from Weight Watchers)

Elva Fisher

1 (24-oz.) lg. can diced tomatoes	1 can Veg-All
1 can green beans	1 can or sm. frozen corn
2 sm. or 1 lg. can vegetable soup	1 can sliced potatoes
	2 cans chili, no beans

Just heat and serve.

PINK SALAD

Marilyn Clayton
From a Tennessee cousin,
Sarah Colene Clayton

1 jar or can cherry pie filling	1 c. nuts, chopped
1 (20-oz.) can chunk or crushed pineapple, drained	1 can Eagle Brand milk
	1 (8 oz.) Cool Whip

Mix pie filling, pineapple, nuts and Eagle Brand milk. Stir and mix well. Add Cool Whip last. Chill and serve. This is oh so good.

SALAD DRESSING

Pearl Sarno

Mix:

¾ c. sugar	1 tsp. dry mustard
1 heaping T. flour	½ tsp. salt

(continued)

Beat 2 whole eggs, add 1 cup milk. Add dry ingredients. Beat and add ½ cup cold water and ½ cup vinegar. Cook in double boiler until thick. Makes a pint and is very good on potato salad.

TACO SALAD

Edwin Watkins

1 head lettuce, chopped
1 bunch green onions, chopped
4 tomatoes, chopped
1 (5½-oz.) pkg. taco chips
12 oz. grated cheddar cheese

1 (15-oz.) can red kidney beans, drained
1 lb. ground beef, browned, drained & chilled

Mix the above ingredients together. Mix 2 cups of salad dressing (Miracle Whip) with Hidden Valley Ranch salad mix. Mix into salad just before serving. Add a few crushed taco chips on top.

STRAWBERRY-BANANA SALAD

Pauline Hoadley

1 (6-oz.) pkg. strawberry gelatin
1 c. boiling water
2 (10-oz.) pkgs. frozen sweetened sliced strawberries, partially thawed
1 (20-oz.) can crushed pineapple, undrained

1 c. mashed firm bananas, about 3 med.
½ to ¾ c. chopped walnuts
2 c. (16 oz.) sour cream
2 tsp. sugar
½ tsp. vanilla extract

In a bowl, dissolve gelatin in water. Stir in strawberries, pineapple, bananas and nuts. Pour half of the mixture into a 13 x 9 x 2-inch dish. Refrigerate for 1 hour or until set. Set the remaining gelatin mixture aside. Combine the sour cream, sugar and vanilla; mix well. Spread over the chilled gelatin. Spoon remaining gelatin mixture over top. Chill overnight. Yields: 12-15 servings.

CRANBERRY SALAD MOLD

Marilyn Clayton

1 (1-lb.) can whole cranberry sauce
1 c. boiling water
1 (3-oz.) pkg. strawberry or cranberry flavored gelatin
1 T. lemon juice

¼ tsp. salt
½ c. Hellmann's real mayonnaise
1 apple, diced
¼ c. chopped walnuts

Heat cranberry sauce; strain. Mix liquid, boiling water and gelatin, stirring until completely dissolved. Add lemon juice and salt. Chill mixture until slightly thickened. Add real mayonnaise (I use light); beat with rotary

(continued)

66230-05

beaten until fluffy. Fold in reserved cranberries, apples and nuts. Stir and chill until slightly thickened. **For candles:** Use assorted sized vessels. Fill sauce can ³/₄ full for largest candle. Spoon remaining mixture into assorted cans or glasses. Chill until firm. Insert birthday candle halves into unmolded candles. I just use a gelatin mold (Tupperware).

FRUIT SALAD

Mary Ann Ballard
Leesburg, FL

1 (11-oz.) can mandarin oranges, drained
1 (20-oz.) can pineapple tidbits, drained
1 (16-oz.) can sliced peaches, drained & cut into bite size pieces

3 bananas, sliced
2 Delicious apples, cut into bite-size pieces
1 c. maraschino cherries
1 c. whole pecans, opt.

Fruit Sauce:

1 (3.4-oz.) pkg. instant French vanilla pudding mix
1 c. cold milk
¹/₃ c. frozen orange juice concentrate, thawed & undiluted

³/₄ c. sour cream

In a large bowl, combine all fruit, which has been well drained. Mix together gently; set aside. For sauce, combine all those ingredients in another bowl. Beat with a wire whisk until smooth (mixture will thicken). Gently fold sauce into fruit. Cover and chill for 3-4 hours before serving.

ONION-CUCUMBER SALAD

Myrna Miller

¹/₄ c. vegetable oil
2 T. vinegar
2 T. sugar
1 T. water

¹/₂ c. sour cream
Salt to taste
1 lg. cucumber, sliced
1 med. red onion, sliced

In a bowl, combine oil, vinegar, sugar, water, sour cream and salt. Add cucumber and onion, toss to coast. Refrigerate several hours or overnight. Yields: 4 to 6 servings.

QUICK CRANBERRY SALAD

Myrna Miller

1 lg. pkg. raspberry Jello
2 pkgs. cranberries
1 tall can crushed pineapple,
  drained

3 c. sugar
1 c. chopped pecans

Wash and grind cranberries. Dissolve Jello in 1 pint hot water, add sugar at same time. Pour in ground berries, add pineapple and pecans. Stir well, place in refrigerator till Jello sets.

10 LAYER SALAD

Ruth Magner

Chopped romaine
Slivered carrots
Green onions
Red pepper
Yellow pepper

Pickles, sliced fine
Tomatoes
Broccoli tops
Radishes, slivered
Frozen peas

Layer; top with Marzetti's buttermilk dressing. Top with shredded cheese.

HAWAIIAN CHICKEN SALAD

Mary Hoadley

2½ c. diced cooked chicken
1 (20-oz.) can pineapple tidbits,
  drained
1 c. seedless red grapes, halved
¾ c. sliced celery
¾ c. mayonnaise

½ tsp. salt
¼ tsp. pepper
1 c. navel orange segments
¾ c. sliced firm bananas
⅓ c. salted peanuts

In a bowl, combine the first seven ingredients. Fold in oranges. Cover and refrigerate until chilled. Just before serving, fold in bananas and sprinkle with peanuts. Yields: 8 servings.

66230-05

CHICKEN SALAD

Pauline Hoadley

Salad:

3 chicken breasts, cooked & diced
1 c. celery, diced
¼ c. green pepper, diced

2 tsp. onion, chopped fine
⅔ c. walnuts, chopped
2 c. white seedless grapes, cut in half

Dressing:

¼ c. half & half cream
1 tsp. salt
⅛ tsp. pepper

2 T. white vinegar
⅔ c. Miracle Whip

Garnish with olives or parsley. Sprinkle top with paprika. Can be served in a hollowed out cantaloupe half.

SWEET & SOUR COLESLAW WITH APPLES

Pauline Hoadley

1 sm. head (2 lbs.) green cabbage, quartered, cored & finely shredded (about 10 c.)
⅓ c. sugar
1½ tsp. salt
⅓ c. cider vinegar

3 T. oil
2 lg. carrots, shredded
2 red apples, quartered, cored & thinly sliced
½ c. each golden raisins & unsalted peanuts

Toss cabbage with sugar and 1 teaspoon salt in a large colander set over a bowl. Let stand 1 to 2 hours to release cabbage liquid. Pat cabbage dry with paper towels and discard any liquid in bowl. Whisk remaining ½ teaspoon salt, the vinegar and oil in a serving bowl to blend. Add cabbage and carrots; toss to coat. Cover and refrigerate at least 2 hours for flavors to blend or overnight. **To serve:** Add apples, raisins and peanuts; toss to mix. Serves 8.

MEXICAN SALAD

Donna Swagler

1 onion
4 tomatoes
1 head lettuce
4 oz. grated cheddar cheese
8 oz. French dressing

2 c. Doritos chips
1 lb. ground beef
15-oz. can kidney beans, drained
¼ tsp. salt

Chop onion, tomato and lettuce, put in large bowl. Toss in cheese and dressing. Crunch and add chips. Brown ground beef. Add kidney beans and salt, then simmer for 10 minutes. Mix into cold salad and serve.

PEA SALAD

Pauline Hoadley

6 T. salad dressing
1/4 c. lemon juice
1/2 c. minced green onion
2 c. frozen peas
1 c. cubed cheddar cheese

1/8 tsp. salt
1/8 tsp. pepper
8 slices bacon, cooked &
  crumbled
2 eggs, chopped fine

One day before serving, combine all ingredients except bacon in a medium bowl. Cover and refrigerate. Just before serving add bacon and mix well. Ham or Spam can be used instead of bacon.

CRANBERRY SALAD

Ruth Eisenlohr

1 lb. cranberries
1/2 c. sugar
1 c. grapes
1 (No. 2) can crushed pineapple,
  drained

1 3/4 c. water
2 pkgs. cherry Jello
1 c. chopped celery

Bring cranberries to a boil with water. Let boil 5 minutes. Beat to break up cranberries, add sugar and Jello. Let stand to partially thickened. Add grapes, celery and pineapple and let set. Break up 1 (3-ounce) package cream cheese and add 1 cup small marshmallows and 1 carton whipped cream. Let stand overnight. In the morning whip and put over Jello cranberries.

TAFFY APPLE SALAD

Dean Jones

1 lg. can crushed pineapple
1 (8 oz.) Cool Whip
2 c. mini marshmallows, white
  or colored
2 c. diced apples with peel on

1 c. dry roasted peanuts
1/2 c. sugar
1 T. flour
1 1/4 T. white vinegar
1 egg

Drain juice from pineapple into saucepan. Add sugar, flour, vinegar and egg. Stir together and cover over medium heat until thickened. Cool. Mix sauce with pineapple, Cool Whip, marshmallows, apples and peanuts. Chill before serving.

66230-05

ORANGE SALAD

Marilyn Clayton
From a cousin,
Reba Smith

1 (8-oz.) ctn. Cool Whip
1 (8-oz.) ctn. cottage cheese
1 (20-oz.) can crushed
  pineapple, drained

1 (11-oz.) can mandarin
  oranges, drained
2 sm. or 1 lg. orange Jello

Mix cottage cheese, pineapple, mandarin oranges and dry Jello. Stir and mix well. Fold in Cool Whip last. Chill and serve.

PRAIRIE PEA SALAD

Dean Jones

6 T. mayonnaise
1/2 c. minced green onions
2 c. frozen peas, unthawed
1 c. cubed or shredded cheddar
  cheese

1/8 tsp. salt
1/8 tsp. pepper
2 hard-boiled eggs, chopped
8 slices bacon, cooked &
  crumbled

One day before serving, combine all ingredients except bacon in medium bowl. Cover and refrigerate. Just before serving add bacon; toss well.

5-CUP SALAD

Hannah Baldwin

1 c. crushed pineapple, drained
1 c. mini marshmallows
1 c. shredded coconut

1 c. mandarin oranges, drained
1 c. sour cream

RED & GREEN SALAD

Connie Castor

1 can French-style green beans
1 can peas
1 jar pimento

1 med. onion
1 green pepper
5 sticks celery

Drain canned vegetables and dice fresh vegetables. Put in glass baking dish and cover with salt (generous). Let stand at least 2 hours. Rinse off salt with cold water and drain.

Pour dressing of:

1/2 c. oil
1 1/2 c. sugar

1 c. vinegar
2 T. water

(continued)

Beat together. Pour over the vegetables and let stand at least overnight. Will keep over the complete holiday season as long as you keep refrigerated. Goes well with most meats.

COLESLAW

Elva Fisher

Shred:

8 c. cabbage	2 carrots

Chop:

1 lg. onion	1 green pepper
1½ c. sugar	1 tsp. dry mustard, opt.
1 c. white vinegar	1 tsp. celery seed
¾ c. salad oil	Salt to taste

Mix cabbage, carrots, onion and green pepper in mixing bowl. Bring remaining ingredients to boil and simmer. Pour over cabbage mixture. Cover and let stand at room temperature for 3 hours. Refrigerate. Keeps 6 weeks.

GREEK STYLE CHICKEN SALAD

Hannah Baldwin

1 (10-oz.) can Valley Fresh premium chunk white chicken, drained, cut into bite-size pieces	1 c. grape-style tomatoes
	1 c. diced cucumbers, with peel
	½ c. sliced red onions
	3 c. cooked tri-color rotini pasta, chilled
1 c. crumbled feta cheese	
1 (3.25-oz.) can sliced ripe black olives	

Dressing:

½ c. olive oil	1 tsp. mined garlic
½ c. white wine vinegar	1 tsp. dried oregano leaves
1 T. lemon juice	½ tsp. salt

Combine pasta, chicken, vegetables, cheese and olives. Mix together dressing ingredients. Pour dressing over pasta mixture and lightly toss until coated with dressing. Chill until ready to serve. Serves 6-8.

66230-05

VEGETABLES & SIDE DISHES

*Blessed are those who hunger
and thirst for righteousness,
for they will be filled.*

~ Matthew 5:6

Helpful Hints

- When preparing a casserole, make an additional batch to freeze. It makes a great emergency meal when unexpected guests arrive. Just take the casserole from the freezer and bake it in the oven.

- To keep hot oil from splattering, sprinkle a little salt or flour in the pan before frying.

- Never overcook foods that are to be frozen. Foods will finish cooking when reheated. Don't refreeze cooked thawed foods.

- A few drops of lemon juice added to simmering rice will keep the grains separated.

- Green pepper may change the flavor of frozen casseroles. Clove, garlic, and pepper flavors get stronger when they are frozen, while sage, onion, and salt get milder.

- Don't freeze cooked egg whites; they become tough.

- For an easy no-mess side dish, grill vegetables along with your meat.

- When freezing foods, label each container with its contents and the date it was put into the freezer. Store at 0°. Always use frozen cooked foods within one to two months.

- Store dried pasta, rice (except brown rice), and whole grains in tightly covered containers in a cool, dry place. Always refrigerate brown rice, and refrigerate or freeze grains if they will not be used within five months.

- To dress up buttered, cooked vegetables, sprinkle them with toasted sesame seeds, toasted chopped nuts, canned french-fried onions, or slightly crushed seasoned croutons.

- Soufflé dishes are designed with straight sides to help your soufflé climb to magnificent heights. Ramekins are good for serving individual casseroles.

- A little vinegar or lemon juice added to potatoes before draining will make them extra white when mashed.

- To quickly bake potatoes, place them in boiling water for 10 to 15 minutes. Pierce their skins with a fork and bake in a preheated oven.

- To avoid toughened beans or corn, add salt midway through cooking.

VEGETABLES & SIDE DISHES

BROCCOLI CASSEROLE

Mary Ann Ballard
Lessburg, FL

2 (10-oz.) boxes frozen, chopped broccoli, cooked & drained	1 sm. to med. chopped onion
1 can cream of mushroom soup	1 (8 oz.) chicken Stove Top stuffing mix
1 c. sour cream	½ c. butter or margarine, melted

Combine first four ingredients in a large bowl; mix well. In another bowl, combine stuffing and butter or margarine; mix well. Place one-half of stuffing mix into a 13 x 9-inch greased casserole dish. Top with broccoli mixture. Top above with remaining stuffing mix. Bake in a preheated 350° oven for 30 minutes until golden brown.

BROCCOLI, RICE & CHEESE

Judy Burch

¼ lb. margarine (1 stick)	1 c. rice
8 oz. Cheez Whiz	2 (10-oz.) pkgs. chopped frozen broccoli
1 onion, chopped	
1 can cream of mushroom soup	

Cook rice according to directions. Combine all ingredients. Salt and pepper to taste. Bake 350° for 20 minutes.

RICE BROCCOLI DISH

Judy Burch

1 c. uncooked Minute Rice	3 T. butter or margarine
1 pkg. chopped broccoli, thawed	½ c. onion, chopped
1 (12-oz.) can cream of chicken soup	½ c. celery, diced
	1 (8-oz.) jar Kraft Cheez Whiz
½ c. milk	1 can water chestnuts, sliced

Mix all ingredients together in a shallow casserole dish. Bake covered at 350° for 30 to 40 minutes, then uncovered for another 10 minutes.

COWBOY BEANS

Jean Sharp

½ lb. hamburger or sausage	½ c. brown sugar
½ lb. bacon	½ c. sugar
¾ c. onion, chopped	1 tsp. salt
No. 2 can pork & beans	½ c. catsup
No. 2 can kidney beans, drained	1 tsp. dry mustard
No. 2 can lima beans, drained	2 T. vinegar
No. 2. can butter beans, drained	

Brown hamburger and bacon; drain. Add onions and beans. Add brown sugar, granulated sugar, salt, catsup, dry mustard and vinegar. Put in casserole dish and bake in 350° oven for 40 minutes.

BAKED BEANS

Dean Jones

1 lb. ground turkey or ground beef	¼ c. brown sugar, packed
1 c. chopped onions	1 tsp. salt
1 (9-oz.) frozen baby lima beans	⅛ tsp. pepper
1 (16-oz.) Bush's baked beans, undrained	1 tsp. mustard
1 (15.5 oz.) kidney beans, drained	½ c. catsup
	2 T. molasses
	1 T. vinegar

Brown ground turkey (or beef) and onions. Drain off fat. Add lima beans and cook until tender. Add remaining ingredients. Pour in baking dish and bake in 350° oven for 35 minutes.

CHEESE FRIED ZUCCHINI

Irene Blakemore

In a plastic bag or shallow bowl, combine ¼ cup dry bread crumbs, 2 tablespoons grated Parmesan cheese, 2 tablespoons flour and 1 teaspoon salt. Thinly slice two medium sized zucchini. Dip zucchini into a well beaten egg, then coat with bread crumb mixture. Fry zucchini in 2 to 4 tablespoons hot vegetable or olive oil until golden brown and crispy (turn occasionally). Drain on paper towels and serve. Makes 3 to 4 servings.

66230-05

3 BEAN BAKE

Pauline Hoadley

1 can baked beans
1 can green lima beans or butter beans
1 can kidney beans
1 c. celery, chopped
1 c. bell pepper, chopped
1 c. onion, chopped

¼ c. catsup
¼ c. barbecue sauce
¼ c. brown sugar
¼ c. vinegar
½ lb. bacon, cut in small pieces, cooked & drained

Mix and bake at 350° for 30-45 minutes.

BAKED CORN

Pauline Hoadley

2 cans cream corn
1 corn muffin mix
1 c. sour cream

3 eggs
1 stick oleo, melted
2 T. sugar

Bake 1 hour or till done at 350°.

SQUASH & SAUSAGE

Pauline Hoadley

½ lb. fully cooked smoked sausage, cut into ¼ inch slices
1 T. olive oil
1 med. zucchini, cut into ¼-inch slices

1 med. yellow summer squash, cut into ¼-inch slices
2 T. apricot preserves

In large skillet, sauté sausage in oil until lightly browned; remove and keep warm. In same skillet, sauté zucchini and yellow squash until crisp and tender. Return sausage to pan. Stir in preserves. Cook and stir until heated through.

SQUASH FRITTERS

Pauline Hoadley

3 c. grated squash
3 T. grated onion
½ c. flour
1½ tsp. salt

1 T. sugar
3 eggs
3 T. butter or margarine

Mix together. Spoon into hot butter or margarine. Fry until brown, 1 to 3 minutes each side.

ZUCCHINI CASSEROLE

Sandy Whaley

4 c. zucchini, chopped	1 can cream of chicken soup
1 stick margarine	½ c. sour cream
2 carrots, diced	1 box chicken Stove Top, dry
2 sm. onions, diced	

Sauté onions and carrots in margarine. Mix all above together put in 9 x 13-inch pan. Bake 350°, 40 minutes.

BROCCOLI PUFF

Pauline Hoadley

1 (10-oz.) pkg. frozen broccoli cuts	¼ c. milk
1 (10½-oz.) can condensed cream of mushroom soup	¼ c. salad dressing
	1 egg, beaten
½ c. (2 oz.) shredded sharp process American cheese	¼ c. fine dry bread crumbs
	1 T. butter or margarine, melted

Cook frozen broccoli according to package, omitting salt; drain thoroughly. Place in 10 x 6 x 1½-inch) baking dish. Mix soup with cheese, add milk, salad dressing and beaten egg to soup mixture; stirring until it is well blended. Pour over broccoli. Combine bread crumbs with melted butter, sprinkle evenly over mixture. Bake until crumbs are lightly browned. Serves 4 to 6.

Recipe Favorites

66230-05

MAIN
DISHES

The Lord loves righteousness and justice;
the earth is full of his unfailing Love.

~ Psalm 33:5

Helpful Hints

- Use little oil when preparing sauces and marinades for red meats. Fat from the meat will render out during cooking and will provide plenty of flavor. Certain meats, like ribs and pot roast, can be parboiled before grilling to reduce the fat content.

- When trying to reduce your fat intake, buy the leanest cuts you can find. Fat will show up as an opaque white coating or can also run through the meat fibers, as marbling. Although most of the fat (the white coating) can be trimmed away, there isn't much that can be done about the marbling. Stay away from well-marbled cuts of meat.

- Home from work late with no time for marinating meat? Pound meat lightly with a mallet or rolling pin, pierce with a fork, sprinkle lightly with meat tenderizer, and add marinade. Refrigerate for about 20 minutes, and you'll have succulent, tender meat.

- Marinating is a cinch if you use a plastic bag. The meat stays in the marinade and it's easy to turn and rearrange. Cleanup is easy; just toss the bag.

- It's easier to thinly slice meat if it's partially frozen.

- Tomatoes added to roasts will help to naturally tenderize them. Tomatoes contain an acid that works well to break down meats.

- Whenever possible, cut meats across the grain; they will be easier to eat and have a better appearance.

- When frying meat, sprinkle paprika over it to turn it golden brown.

- Thaw all meats in the refrigerator for maximum safety.

- Refrigerate poultry promptly after purchasing. Keep it in the coldest section of your refrigerator for up to two days. Freeze poultry for longer storage. Never leave poultry at room temperature for more than two hours.

- If you're microwaving skinned chicken, cover the baking dish with vented clear plastic wrap to keep the chicken moist.

- Lemon juice rubbed on fish before cooking will enhance the flavor and help maintain a good color.

- Scaling a fish is easier if vinegar is rubbed on the scales first.

MAIN DISHES

MARYLIN'S HOT CHICKEN SALAD

Marylin Konkle

2 c. chicken, cooked & cubed
1 c. celery, diced
2 c. rice, cooked
¾ c. mayonnaise
1 c. sliced mushrooms, canned

1 c. water chestnuts, sliced
1 tsp. onion
1 tsp. lemon juice
1 tsp. salt
1 can cream of chicken soup

Mix all ingredients and place in buttered 7 x 11-inch casserole.

Topping:

½ c. margarine, melted
1 pkg. sliced almonds

1 c. crushed cornflakes

Combine and place over casserole. Bake at 35 minutes in 350° oven. Best if made the day before, then baked before serving.

IRISH POTATO CASSEROLE

Marilyn Clayton
From my friend,
Shirley Boone

6 whole Irish potatoes, about
  the size of an orange
½ c. melted margarine or butter
2 c. grated cheddar cheese
⅓ c. chopped (or thinly sliced)
  green onions

3 tsp. salt
2 (8-oz.) ctns. sour cream, can
  use light

Boil potatoes. Refrigerate or cool completely. Grate potatoes on a course grater. To potatoes add rest of ingredients. Blend all together and put in greased casserole (3-quart oblong Pyrex dish). Bake at 350° for 30-40 minutes.

BROCCOLI CORN CASSEROLE

Londa Wines

1 (10-oz.) pkg. frozen chopped
  broccoli, thawed
1 (14¾-oz.) can cream-style
  corn

1 egg
1½ c. stuffing mix
½ c. butter or margarine, melted

In a bowl, combine broccoli, corn and egg. Transfer to a greased 1-quart baking dish. Sprinkle with stuffing mix and drizzle with butter. Bake uncovered at 350° for 30-35 minutes or until golden brown and bubbly. Yields: 6 servings.

BACON TATOR BAKE

Londa Wines

2 (10¾-oz.) cans condensed
  cream of mushroom soup,
  undiluted
1⅓ c. sour cream

1 lg. onion, chopped
1 lb. sliced bacon, cooked &
  crumbled
1 (32-oz.) pkg. frozen Tater Tots

In a large bowl, combine the soup, sour cream and onion. Add the bacon and Tater Tots, stir until combined. Transfer to a greased 13 x 9 x 2-inch baking dish. Cover and bake at 350° for 50 minutes. Uncover and bake 8-10 minutes longer or until golden brown. Yields: 10 servings.

TANGY PARTY MEATBALLS

Londa Wines

Mix together lightly:

1 c. cornflakes, mashed
2 lbs. hamburger
2 T. onion flakes
2 T. soy sauce

¼ tsp. black pepper
½ tsp. garlic powder
2 eggs, slightly beaten
½ c. ketchup

Gently roll into firm small balls (1½ inch, size of medium walnut). Set aside. Prepare sauce using 12 ounces chili sauce, 16 ounces cranberry sauce, 2 tablespoons sugar and 2 tablespoon lemon juice. Place meatballs with sauce in 9 x 13-inch baking dish. Bake 35-40 minutes at 400° oven.

BEEF STROGANOFF

Bob Wines

Brown together in pan:

1½ lbs. hamburger
½ c. green pepper
½ c. onion
½ c. celery

8 strips bacon, cut in small
  pieces
1 can mushrooms

When hamburger and bacon are done:

Add:

2 cans mushroom soup

1 (16-oz.) tub sour cream

Stir together.

**Spices to be added to your
taste:**

**Garlic powder
Celery seed**

Salt & pepper

Cook noodles and serve.

16

HONEY BARBEQUE MEAT LOAF

Marylin Konkle

1 tsp. beef bouillon granules
1 T. hot water
1 egg
½ c. quick-cooking oats
⅓ c. honey barbecue sauce
¼ c. chopped onion
2 T. brown sugar
1 T. Worcestershire sauce

1 T. prepared mustard
½ tsp. garlic powder
¼ tsp. salt
½ tsp. pepper
¼ tsp. chili powder
1 lb. ground beef
Ketchup

In large bowl, dissolve bouillon in hot water. Stir in egg, oatmeal, barbecue sauce, onion, brown sugar, Worcestershire sauce, mustard, garlic powder, chili pepper, salt, pepper. Add beef and mix well. Press into greased 8 x 4 x 2-inch pan. Bake for 1 hour at 350°. Let stand 10 minutes. Top with ketchup and bake 5 to 10 minutes more. Serves 4-6.

SIX-VEGGIE CASSEROLE

1 (16-oz.) pkg. frozen cut green
  beans, thawed
2 c. sliced celery
1½ c. sliced carrots
1½ c. sliced onions
¾ c. sliced green pepper
1 (14½-oz.) can diced tomatoes,
  undrained

¼ c. butter, melted
3 T. quick-cooking tapioca
1 T. sugar
1 tsp. salt
½ tsp. pepper
1 (2.8-oz.) can French-fried
  onions

In large bowl, combine the beans, celery, carrots, onion, green pepper and tomatoes. Add butter, tapioca, sugar, salt and pepper; mix well. Transfer to an ungreased 2½-quart baking dish. Cover and bake at 350° for 50 minutes. Uncover; sprinkle with French-fried onions. Bake 20 minutes longer or until vegetables are tender. Yields: 12-14 servings.

PARTY MEATBALLS

Dean Jones

2 lbs. ground beef
⅓ c. dried parsley
½ tsp. garlic powder
2 T. instant onions
1 c. cornflake crumbs

2 eggs
1 T. soy sauce
⅓ c. catsup
¼ tsp. pepper

Mix thoroughly and form into little balls and pour sauce over them.

(continued)

Sauce:

1 (1-lb.) can jellied cranberry
  sauce
1 (12-oz.) bottle chili sauce

2 T. brown sugar
1 T. lemon juice

Heat mixture till cranberry sauce melts. Bake in 350° oven 30 minutes.
Serves 90.

CASHEW CHICKEN

Hannah Baldwin

1 lb. boneless, skinless chicken
  breasts, cut into 1-inch cubes
1 med. onion, chopped
2 c. frozen broccoli cuts
1¾ c. boiling water
1 c. uncooked long-grain rice

1 (6-oz.) jar sliced mushrooms,
  drained
1 T. chicken bouillon granules
½ to 1 tsp. ground ginger
Pepper, to taste
¾ c. salted cashews, divided

In large bowl, combine the first 9 ingredients. Transfer to a greased
shallow 1½-quart baking dish. Cover and bake at 375° for 45-55 minutes or until rice is tender and chicken is no longer pink. Stir in ½ cup
of cashews. Sprinkle with remaining cashews. Looks very good. Yields:
4 servings.

CHICKEN-OLIVE-CHEDDAR QUICHE

Hannah Baldwin

½ (15-oz.) pkg. pie crusts
2 c. chopped grilled chicken
1 (8-oz.) can sliced mushrooms,
  drained
2 to 3 green onions, chopped
2 T. sliced black olives
1 garlic clove, minced
2 T. chopped fresh or 1 tsp.
  dried basil

¼ tsp. ground red pepper
Vegetable cooking spray
1 c. (4 oz.) shredded cheddar
  cheese
1 c. half & half
4 eggs
¼ tsp. pepper

Sauté: Chicken and next 6 ingredients in a skillet coated with cooking
spray over medium-high heat 5 minutes. Spoon mixture into prepared
crust. Sprinkle with cheese. **Whisk** together half & half, eggs, 2¼ teaspoons pepper. Pour over chicken mixture. Bake at 400° on lowest
oven rack for 45 minutes or until set. Let stand 10 minutes.

18

HAM 'N CHEESE QUICHE

Hannah Baldwin

2 (9-inch) pastry shells
2 c. diced fully cooked ham
2 c. (8 oz.) shredded sharp
  cheddar cheese
2 tsp. dried minced onion

4 eggs
2 c. half & half cream
½ tsp. salt
¼ tsp. pepper

Line unpricked pastry shells with a double thickness of heavy-duty foil. Bake at 400° for 5 minutes. Remove foil; bake 5 minutes longer. Divide ham, cheese and onion between the shells. In a bowl, whisk eggs, cream, salt and pepper. Pour into shells. Cover edges with foil and bake at 400° for 35-40 minutes or until a knife inserted near the center comes out clean. Let stand for 5-10 minutes before cutting.

HASH BROWN CASSEROLE

Hannah Baldwin

½ c. margarine
2 lbs. southern hash browns
1 pt. sour cream
1 can cream of chicken soup
2 c. shredded cheddar cheese

½ c. chopped onion
½ tsp. pepper
½ tsp. salt
1 c. crushed cornflakes to
  sprinkle on top

Cook uncovered in a baking dish for 1½ hours at 350°. You can also add green pepper.

MEMPHIS HAMBURGER PIE

Hannah Baldwin

1 lb. ground beef
½ c. chopped onion
½ tsp. salt
Dash pepper
1 can green beans, drained
1 can tomato soup

5 med. potatoes, cooked
½ c. milk
1 egg, beaten
½ c. American cheese,
  shredded

Cook ground beef and onion until lightly browned and onion is tender. Add salt, pepper, beans and soup. Pour into a greased 1½-quart casserole. Mash potatoes, while hot add egg and milk.

CHICKEN PICCATA

Hannah Baldwin

Whole chicken, cut up
1 egg
3 T. lemon juice
1/4 c. flour
1/2 tsp. garlic powder

1/4 tsp. paprika, opt.
1/4 c. butter or margarine
2 chicken bouillon cubes
1/2 c. boiling water

Beat egg with 1 tablespoon lemon juice. Combine flour, garlic powder and paprika. Dip chicken in egg then flour mix. In skillet, brown chicken in butter or margarine. Dissolve bouillon cube in water, add remaining lemon juice. Pour over chicken. Simmer 20 minutes.

MEAT LOVERS PIZZA BAKE

*Carol Oakes
from Sturgis, MI*

1 lb. ground beef
1/2 c. chopped green pepper
1 (15-oz.) can pizza sauce
1 (3 1/2-oz.) pkg. sliced pepperoni, chopped
1 (2 1/4-oz.) can sliced ripe olives, drained

2 c. (8 oz.) shredded mozzarella cheese
3/4 c. biscuit/baking mix
2 eggs
3/4 c. milk

In a large skillet, cook beef and green pepper over medium heat until meat is no longer pink; drain. Stir in the pizza sauce, pepperoni and olives. Transfer to a greased 11 x 7 x 2-inch baking dish. Sprinkle with cheese. In a small bowl, combine the biscuit mix, eggs and milk until blended. Pour evenly over cheese. Bake uncovered at 400° for 25-30 minutes or until golden brown. Let stand for 10 minutes before serving. Yields: 6 servings. Preparation time: 20 minutes. Bake: 25 minutes + standing.

HURRY-UP CASSEROLE

Dorothy Davis Bangor

1 (8-oz.) jar or 1 c. Cheez Whiz
2 can (condensed) cream of chicken soup
1/2 c. milk
1/2 c. chopped onion
4 T. butter

2 (10-oz.) pkgs. frozen chopped broccoli
4 c. diced cooked ham
2 c. pre-cooked rice (Minute)
1/2 tsp. Worcestershire sauce, opt.

Blend cheese, soup and milk, cook onion in butter until tender. Cook broccoli until tender and drain. Mix all ingredients in 2 1/2-quart casserole. Cover and bake at 350° for 30 minutes. Yields: 8 servings.

66230-05

REUBEN CASSEROLE

Dorothy Davis

2 (27-oz.) cans sauerkraut
16 oz. thin sliced corned beef,
  cut into bite-size pieces

1 c. Thousand Island dressing
2 c. shredded Swiss cheese
6-8 rye bread, large pieces

Mix all ingredients together well and place in buttered baking dish. Bake at 350° for 40-45 minutes. Serves 12 or divide into 2 baking dishes for 2 servings of six.

THAT

Women's Circle magazine
Marilyn Clayton

1 lb. hamburger or Morningstar
  crumbles
4 med. potatoes
1 sm. onion, sliced

2 tsp. salt
1 tsp. Accent, opt.
1 can green beans or 1 pkg.
  frozen green beans

Cook hamburger slowly in skillet until evenly browned, stirring frequently. Pour off any accumulated grease. Add sliced onion, potatoes which have been scrubbed and cut in 1-inch pieces, beans and seasonings. If frozen beans are used, add ¾ cup water. If canned beans are used, add liquid with the beans. Stir to distribute seasoning, cover skillet and cook until tender, 20-30 minutes.

ZESTY ITALIAN CASSEROLE

1 lb. ground beef, cooked &
  drained
1 can mushrooms, drained
½ jar spaghetti sauce
2 T. sour cream
8 oz. shredded mozzarella
  cheese

1 pkg. crescents from the dairy
  case
Parmesan cheese
Melted butter

Combine hamburger, mushrooms and spaghetti sauce. Pour into casserole baking dish. Spread sour cream over mixture and top with mozzarella cheese. Spread out crescents and layer over top. Brush lightly with butter and sprinkle Parmesan cheese over top. Bake at 350° for 20-25 minutes. Serves three or four.

SWEET & SOUR CHICKEN

Pauline Hoadley

1 lb. boneless chicken breasts
¾ c. fat-free chicken broth
1 (15¼-oz.) can pineapple
  chunks in juice
1 green pepper, cut in thin
  strips
1 red pepper, cut in thin strips

1 carrot, sliced diagonally
¼ c. vinegar
2 tsp. sugar
1 T. cornstarch
2 T. soy sauce
3 c. hot cooked rice

Cut chicken into 1-inch cubes. Heat chicken broth to boiling in large skillet, add chicken. Simmer 5 to 10 minutes, stirring occasionally. Add undrained pineapple chunks, green and red pepper, carrot, vinegar and sugar; bring to a boil. Stir cornstarch into soy sauce until smooth, stir into skillet mixture. Bring to boiling, stirring constantly. Lower heat, cover, simmer 10 minutes. Serve over hot cooked rice. Makes 4 servings.

CASSEROLE DISH

Catherine Wildt

1 lb. hamburger
½ c. cut-up onion

1 c. cut-up celery

Fry all together till meat isn't pink and add:

2 cans mushroom soup
  (creamed)

1½ c. water
½ c. rice

Mix well and put in casserole dish and bake 1 hour at 350°. Onion rings can be put on top if desired and baked 15 minutes more.

HAWAIIAN CHICKEN WINGS

Joan Sharp

2 lbs. wingettes or drumettes
1 c. soy sauce
½ c. brown sugar
2-3 cloves garlic, minced

1 T. sesame oil
2 T. sesame seeds
4 green onions, chopped

Flour chicken the night before and store in paper bag in refrigerator. Fry wings in 1 inch oil to light brown. Cool. Mix soy sauce, sugar, garlic, oil, sesame seeds and onions. Dip wings in sauce and place on cookie sheet. Warm in oven to set sauce and reheat wings.

66230-05

SCALLOPED CHICKEN SUPPER

Cheryl Maczko

1 (4.9-oz.) pkg. scalloped
 potatoes
1/8 tsp. poultry seasoning
1 3/4 c. boiling water
1 (10 3/4-oz.) can condensed
 cream of chicken soup,
 undiluted

2 c. cubed cooked chicken
1 c. shredded carrots
1/2 c. chopped celery
1/4 c. finely chopped onion

Set the potatoes aside. Place the contents of the sauce mix in a large bowl; sprinkle with poultry seasoning. Whisk in the water and soup. Stir in the chicken, carrots, celery, onion and potatoes. Transfer to a greased 2-quart baking dish. Bake uncovered at 400° for 45-50 minutes or until vegetables are tender. Yields: 4 servings. Preparation time: 10 minutes. Bake: 45 minutes.

HAM BALLS IN PINEAPPLE SAUCE

Ruth Eisenlohr

2 lbs. ground ham & 2 lbs.
 ground pork, together

4 eggs
2 c. bread crumbs, soft

Combine ingredients, form into balls and place in shallow pan. Bake in 350° oven for 25 minutes.

Sauce:

2 cans crushed pineapple
2/3 c. catsup
2/3 c. vinegar

1/4 c. soy sauce
1 c. brown sugar

Mix together and pour over meatballs when they have baked 25 minutes.

MEATBALLS

3 lbs. ground beef
6 T. Worcestershire sauce
1 pkg. onion soup mix, dry

1 lg. can evaporated milk, like
 Carnation

Mix about ingredients, let stand 5 minutes. Form into balls. Bake on cookie sheet or baking pan for 15 to 20 minutes in 400° oven.

Sauce:

1 T. Worcestershire sauce
2 c. catsup

3/4 c. brown sugar, packed

Mix ingredients into saucepan and heat until sugar is melted. Pour over meatballs in crockpot and simmer. Good.

RAVIOLI

Grace Shields

2 cans Chef Boy-Ar-Dee ravioli with meat	2 cans mushroom soup
1 lb. chopped beef	Parmesan cheese
	Cracker meal

Brown meat in fry pan. Place in bottom of glass baking dish. Cover with raviolis, separated carefully. Spread mushroom soup over all, return to refrigerator until you wish to use. This can be kept for a couple of days. When you wish to use it sprinkle with cracker meal. Place in oven at 400°, bake until it is thoroughly heated. It will bubble around edges. Serve with cheese.

SUPER BURGERS

Hannah Baldwin

1 lb. ground beef	½ tsp. Worcestershire sauce
1 T. flour	1 pkg. onion soup mix

Brown meat, blend flour, add Worcestershire sauce, 3 cans water, onion soup mix. Simmer for 20 minutes. Eat over buns.

SAT. NIGHT SPREAD

Hannah Baldwin

1 lb. ground beef, cook until done	2 T. ketchup
½ c. onion	2 T. mustard
1 can chicken gumbo soup	Salt & pepper

Simmer everything over low heat for 20 minutes.

OPEN FACE HAMBURGERS

Virginia Kenney

Mix together:

1 lb. ground chuck	2 T. chili sauce
1 sm. onion, diced	⅜ lb. Velveeta, cubed & spread
¼ green pepper, diced	on half a bun
2 T. mustard	

Bake at 350° for 10-15 minutes. Extra meat mixture can be frozen. Serves 7 or 14 halves.

66230-05

BEEF & POTATO BAKE

Luelloa Pumfery

1 lb. ground beef
¼ c. minced onion
¼ c. minced celery
¼ c. chili sauce
1 egg
Butter

¼ tsp. paprika
¼ tsp. pepper
2¼ c. instant potatoes
Milk
Salt

Mix beef, onion, celery, chili sauce, egg, pepper and half of potato flakes, ¾ cup milk and 1½ teaspoon salt together. Spread in 9-inch pie plate. Bake at 350° for 35 minutes. Prepare remaining potato flakes as label directs. When meat is done, spread the mashed potatoes on meat. Dot with butter, sprinkle with paprika and broil 3 minutes until potatoes are golden brown. Yields: 4 servings.

TUNA CASSEROLE

1 (6-oz.) can tuna
2 T. celery
2 T. green pepper
2 T. onion
2 eggs, beaten

1½ c. cottage cheese
1 c. bread crumbs
2 T. margarine
Sm. can mushrooms
¼ c. Parmesan cheese

Grease casserole, mix all together in casserole and sprinkle cheese on top. Bake at 350° for 1 hour.

BAKED SWISS STEAK

Mary Ann Ballard
Leesburg, FL

½ to ¾ lb. boneless round
 steak
2 T. all-purpose flour, divided
½ tsp. salt
2 T. vegetable oil
1 (14½-oz.) can stewed
 tomatoes

½ c. chopped carrot
¼ c. chopped celery
1 T. chopped onion
¼ tsp. Worcestershire sauce
2 T. sharp cheddar cheese

Cut meat into two portions: pound to ¼ inch thickness. Combine 1 tablespoon flour and the salt; coat meat on both sides. In a skillet, brown meat in oil. Transfer meat to a greased shallow 2-quart baking dish; set aside. To pan drippings, add tomatoes, carrot, celery, onion, Worcestershire sauce and remaining flour. Bring to a boil over medium heat; cook and stir 2 minutes. Pour over meat. Cover and bake at 350° for 1½ hours or until meat is tender. Sprinkle with cheese; return to oven until cheese is melted.

SLOPPY JOES

Dean Jones

1½ lbs. ground beef
1 sm. onion, chopped
1 sm. green pepper, chopped
1 (10¾-oz.) tomato soup,
 undiluted

1 (8 oz.) tomato sauce
2 T. brown sugar
1 T. Worcestershire sauce
1 tsp. prepared mustard
Pinch of garlic powder (⅛ tsp.)

Cook ground beef, onion and green pepper in a large skillet until beef is browned. Drain. Stir in tomato soup and next 5 ingredients. Simmer 10 to 15 minutes (I like to cook it longer) stirring mixture often. Yields: 6.

BUSY DAY STEW

Londa Wines

3 lbs. stew meat
1 pkg. dry onion soup mix
5 carrots
4 stalks celery
5 lg. potatoes, chopped
2 lg. onions, chopped

1 can or 1 bag frozen peas &
 corn
2 cans cream of mushroom
 soup
1 soup can of water
Salt & pepper to taste

Grease 9 x 13-inch pan with butter or cooking spray. Lay the meat in the bottom of the pan and sprinkle with soup mix. Over this, place the veggies in another layer. Pour the 2 cans of soup and 1 can of water over the top. Cover with foil and bake 4 hours at 300° oven.

Recipe Favorites

66230-05

BREADS
& ROLLS

Then Jesus declared, "I am the bread of life. He who comes to me will never go hungry, and he who believes in me will never be thirsty."

~ John 6:35

Helpful Hints

- Over-ripe bananas can be peeled and frozen in a plastic container until it's time to bake bread or cake.

- When baking bread, a small dish of water in the oven will help keep the crust from getting too hard or brown.

- Use shortening, not margarine or oil, to grease pans, as margarine and oil absorb more readily into the dough or batter (especially bread).

- Use a metal ice tray divider to cut biscuits in a hurry. Press into the dough, and biscuits will separate at dividing lines when baked.

- To make self-rising flour, mix 4 cups flour, 2 teaspoons salt, and 2 tablespoons baking powder, and store in a tightly covered container.

- Hot water kills yeast. One way to tell the correct temperature is to pour the water over your forearm. If you cannot feel either hot or cold, the temperature is just right.

- When in doubt, always sift flour before measuring.

- When baking in a glass pan, reduce the oven temperature by 25°.

- When baking bread, you get a finer texture if you use milk. Water makes a coarser bread.

- If your biscuits are dry, it could be from too much handling, or the oven temperature may not have been hot enough.

- Nut breads are better if stored 24 hours before serving.

- To make bread crumbs, toast the heels of bread and chop in a blender or food processor.

- Cracked eggs should not be used because they may contain bacteria.

- The freshness of eggs can be tested by placing them in a large bowl of cold water; if they float, do not use them.

- For a quick, low-fat crunchy topping for muffins, sprinkle the tops with Grape-Nuts cereal before baking.

- Dust a bread pan or work surface with flour by filling an empty glass salt shaker with flour.

BREADS & ROLLS

BREAD DOUGH

Connie Castor

Scald 2 cups milk, add 4 tablespoons oleo and let melt and set aside to cool. Pour ½ cup medium hot water over 2 packages dry yeast and 1 teaspoon sugar. Mix well and let stand till mixture fills small Pyrex bowl. Meanwhile: Beat 3 eggs; add ½ cup sugar and 1 tablespoon salt. When milk mixture is cool and yeast mixture has risen, mix together with egg mixture and add 7 or 8 cups flour. Divide in two and let rise till double. This dough can be used for dinner rolls, breakfast rolls, bread, pizza etc. **Pizza:** When dough is ready, roll out to fit 4 pizza pans. Spread dough with Chef Boy-Ar-Dee spaghetti sauce. Cook sausage before hand, add sausage, mushrooms, green pepper, cheese or whatever your family desires. Sprinkle Parmesan cheese and last of all sprinkle with mozzarella cheese. Let rise 1 hour and bake 20 minutes at 350°.

CRANBERRY BREAD

Pauline Hoadley

Sift together:

2 c. flour	½ tsp. baking soda
1 c. sugar	1 tsp. salt
1½ tsp. baking powder	

Combine:

1 egg, well beaten	1 T. orange rind, grated
¾ c. orange juice	3 T. oil

Mix dry ingredients well. Add egg mixture all at once. Mix only to dampen. Carefully fold in ½ cup nuts, 2 cups coarsely chopped cranberries. Bake at 350° for 1 hour.

DATE NUT BREAD

Hazel Cramer

2 c. boiling water	2 tsp. vanilla
2½ c. (No. 1) pitted dates, cut up	3 c. flour
2 tsp. baking soda	Dash salt
½ c. sugar	2 T. butter, melted
2 eggs	1 c. chopped nuts

Pour boiling water over dates, mix and set aside. Mix soda, sugar, eggs, vanilla, salt and butter. Add in flour, dates, water and nuts. Pour in 2

(continued)

greased, floured loaf pans and bake at 350° for 1 hour. Serve with butter or cream cheese.

PUMPKIN BREAD

Hazel Cramer

3 c. sugar	1½ tsp. salt
1 c. oil	1 tsp. nutmeg
3 eggs	2 tsp. baking soda
⅔ c. water	1 T. baking powder
3 c. flour	2 c. pumpkin
1 tsp. cinnamon	1 c. chopped nuts

Beat together sugar, oil and eggs. Sift together flour, cinnamon, salt, nutmeg, baking soda and baking powder. Add sifted dry ingredients alternately with water, beating after each addition. Add pumpkin, nuts and stir well. Pour into greased loaf pans. Bake at 350° for 90 minutes or until toothpick comes out clean.

BANANA NUT BREAD

Hazel Cramer

½ c. shortening	2 c. flour
1 c. sugar	1 tsp. soda
2 eggs	½ tsp. salt
3 bananas, crushed	1 tsp. cream of tartar
½ c. nuts	

Cream shortening and sugar; add eggs 1 at a time and beat well. Add crushed bananas and nuts. Add flour with soda, salt and cream of tartar (all sifted together). Pour into greased loaf pan. Bake at 350° for 45 minutes. Making 1½ batches then dividing it into 2 loaves works best.

PANCAKES

Dean Jones

1¼ c. flour	1 egg
2½ tsp. baking powder	¾ c. milk
2 T. sugar	3 T. melted oleo or butter

Beat egg, add milk and melted oleo. Add dry ingredients and mix. You may need to add just a little bit more milk if batter is too thick.

66230-05

BLUEBERRY MUFFINS

Lill Gurr

1 c. sugar
2½ c. flour
1 tsp. soda
2 tsp. cream of tartar
½ c. milk

1 egg
½ c. Mazola oil
1 tsp. salt
1 pt. frozen blueberries

Mix dry ingredients; work in oil and add milk gradually, well beaten egg and blueberries. Bake at 350°, 30 minutes. Serves: 20 large.

CRANBERRY FRUIT BREAD

Virginia Kenney

2 c. flour
1 c. sugar
1½ tsp. baking powder
½ tsp. soda
1 tsp. salt

½ c. chopped nuts
Juice & grated rind of 1 orange
2 T. melted shortening
1 egg
2 c. cranberries, cut in halves

Sift together flour, sugar, baking powder, soda and salt. Combine orange juice, grated rind, melted shortening and enough water to make ¾ cup juice. Then stir in beaten egg. Pour this mixture into dry ingredients, mixing just enough to dampen. Fold in cranberries and nuts. Bake in greased loaf pan (9 x 5 x 3 inches). Bake in moderate oven, 350°, 50-60 minutes. Remove from pan, store overnight for easy slicing. This freezes well.

MONKEY BREAD

Edwina Watkins

3 sm. tubes buttermilk biscuits,
 cut into quarters

Roll into ball and coat with cinnamon and sugar. Layer each ball into a tube pan. Add nuts of desired.

1 c. brown sugar
1½ sticks margarine

1 tsp. cinnamon

Melt sugar, margarine and cinnamon together in small saucepan; over biscuits. Bake 350° for 25 to 30 minutes. While still warm flip onto large plate. Great for Sunday breakfast.

ALL SEASON BREAD

Dean Jones

3 c. flour
2 tsp. baking soda
1 tsp. salt
½ tsp. baking powder
1½ tsp. cinnamon
¾ c. chopped nuts
3 eggs

2 c. sugar
¾ c. vegetable oil
2 tsp. vanilla
1 (8-oz.) can crushed pineapple, drained
2 c. fruit or vegetables

Combine flour, soda, salt, baking powder, cinnamon and nuts. Set aside. Beat eggs lightly in a large mixing bowl; add sugar, oil and vanilla. Beat until creamy. Drain pineapple. Add pineapple and 2 cups prepared fruit or vegetable. Add dry ingredients, stirring until they are moistened. Pour batter into 2 well greased loaf pans. Bake at 350° for 1 hour or until wooden pick inserted comes out clean. Cool for 10 minutes before removing from pans. Alternate fruit and vegetable suggestions to make 2 cups:

Apple, peel, core & shred 3 med. apples
Banana, mash 2 large bananas

Carrot, peel & shred 2 med. carrots & add 1 T. juice, drained from pineapple

SOUR CREAM BLUEBERRY BREAD

Londa Wines

2 c. all-purpose flour
1 tsp. baking soda
½ tsp. salt
½ tsp. cinnamon
1 c. butter (2 sticks), softened
¾ c. sugar

2 lg. eggs, slightly beaten
1 c. mashed bananas (2 med.)
½ c. sour cream
1 c. fresh or frozen blueberries
½ c. coarsely chopped nuts

Preheat oven to 350°. Grease and flour 9 x 5-inch loaf pan. Set aside together dry ingredients. Cream butter and sugar, add eggs, bananas and sour cream, beat until blended. Beat in dry ingredients on low speed until smooth. Fold in blueberries and nuts. Bake 1 hour, let cool completely in pan.

BAKED DOUGHNUTS

In memory of Ethel Hunt

1 c. mashed potatoes
1 pkg. yeast
¼ c. warm potato water
1 c. scalded milk
¾ c. shortening

½ c. sugar
1 tsp. salt
2 beaten eggs
4½ c. flour

(continued)

Add shortening, sugar, salt to milk. Cool to lukewarm. Add mashed potatoes, yeast (dissolved in potato water). Blend in egg. Work in flour. Cover, let rise until light. Knead on floured board. Roll dough ½ inch thick. Cut with doughnut cutter (large hole). Place on buttered sheets; rise until light. Bake until delicately brown. Brush all sides with butter and roll in sugar while still warm.

OVEN BAKED FRENCH TOAST

Sandy Whaley

½ c. melted butter, real butter   **1 c. brown sugar**

Mix and put in bottom of 9 x 13-inch pan.

**1 loaf French bread, cut ¾ inch
  thick**

Layer in pan.

Beat together:

6 eggs   **1 tsp. vanilla**
1½ c. whole milk

Pour over French bread; cover and chill overnight. Shake cinnamon on top. Bake 350°, 45 minutes.

BANANA BREAD

Myrna Miller

½ c. butter	**1 egg**
1 c. sugar	**1½ c. flour**
½ tsp. salt	**1 tsp. vanilla**
3-4 ripe bananas	**½ c. nuts**
1 tsp. soda	

Cream butter and sugar. Add egg. Mix well. Mash bananas and add. Sift dry ingredients and add to mixture. Bake in loaf pan 1 hour at 325°.

DOUBLE QUICK DINNER ROLLS

Sandy Whaley

1 c. warm water (110°-115°)	**1 tsp. salt**
1 pkg. dry yeast	**1 egg, slightly beaten**
2 T. sugar	**2 T. soft shortening**
2¼ c. flour	

In large bowl, dissolve yeast and water. Stir sugar, ½ of flour and salt into yeast. Beat with spoon until smooth. Add egg and shortening. Beat in rest of flour until smooth, scraping sides of bowl. Cover with cloth. Let rise in warm place (85°) until double about 30 minutes. Grease 12

(continued)

large muffin cups. Stir down raised dough. Spoon into muffin cups, filling ½ full. Again let rise in warm place until dough reaches tops of muffin cups 20-30 minutes. Bake at 400° for 15-20 minutes.

Recipe Favorites

66230-05

DESSERTS

*Pleasant words are a honeycomb,
sweet to the soul and
healing to the bones.*

~ Proverbs 16:24

Helpful Hints

- Egg whites need to be at room temperature for greater volume when whipped. Remember this when making meringue.

- When preparing several batches of pie dough, roll dough out between sheets of plastic wrap. Stack the discs in a pizza box, and keep the box in the freezer. Pull out the required crusts as needed.

- Place your pie plate on a cake stand when placing the pie dough in it and fluting the edges. The cake stand will make it easier to turn the pie plate, and you won't have to stoop over.

- Many kitchen utensils can be used to make decorative pie edges. For a scalloped edge, use a spoon. Crosshatched and herringbone patterns are achieved with a fork. For a sharply pointed effect, use a can opener to cut out points around the rim.

- Keep strawberries fresh for up to ten days by refrigerating them (unwashed) in an airtight container between layers of paper towels.

- When grating citrus peel, bits of peel are often stuck in the holes of the grater. Rather than waste the peel, you can easily brush it off by using a new, clean toothbrush.

- To core a pear, slice the pear in half lengthwise. Use a melon baller to cut out the central core, using a circular motion. Draw the melon baller to the top of the pear, removing the interior stem as you go.

- When cutting butter into flour for pastry dough, the process is easier if you cut the butter into small pieces before adding it to the flour.

- To keep the cake plate clean while frosting, slide 6-inch strips of waxed paper under each side of the cake. Once the cake is frosted and the frosting is set, pull the strips away leaving a clean plate.

- When decorating a cake with chocolate, you can make a quick decorating tube. Put chocolate in a heat-safe zipper-lock plastic bag. Immerse in simmering water until the chocolate is melted. Snip off the tip of one corner, and squeeze the chocolate out of the bag.

- Professionally decorated cakes have a silky, molten look. To get that appearance, frost your cake as usual, then use a hair dryer to blow-dry the surface until the frosting slightly melts.

- To ensure that you have equal amounts of batter in each pan when making a layered cake, use a kitchen scale to measure the weight.

DESSERTS

PINEAPPLE CAKE

Maude Moore

1 pkg. Jiffy cake mix (yellow or white)

Bake in greased and floured 9 x 13-inch pan at 350° according to directions on package. Let cool. Drain large can crushed pineapple. Put in bowl and add 1 large package Philadelphia cream cheese softened to room temperature, 1 package instant vanilla or French vanilla pudding and pie mix. Blend with electric mixer until smooth and creamy. Put on cake, spread with 1 large Cool Whip and sprinkle with coconut, if desired.

BANKET

Crystal Rooze

Crust:

2 c. flour	7 T. water
½ c. shortening	Salt & sugar, to taste
½ c. butter	

Bake 30 minutes at 400°.

Filling:

2 c. sugar	8 T. milk
6 tsp. almond flavoring	3 egg yolks
8 T. flour	

WALDORF SALAD CAKE

Jean Hansel

2¼ c. flour	1½ c. sugar
1½ tsp. soda	⅔ c. oil
1 tsp. salt	1 tsp. grated lemon peel
1 tsp. cinnamon	2 c. chopped apples
½ tsp. nutmeg	⅓ c. chopped celery
3 lg. eggs	1 c. chopped walnuts

Sift flour with soda, salt and spices. Beat eggs with sugar until thick and light yellow. Add oil and lemon peel. Mix lightly. Add chopped apples and celery. Then flour mixture. Beat on low speed of mixer 2 minutes. Fold in nuts. Turn into well greased and floured 9-inch tube pan. Bake below oven center at 350°, 60 to 65 minutes. Remove from oven, let cake stand in pan 15 minutes then turn out on wire rack until cool. Sprinkle with powdered sugar.

7-UP CAKE

Lill Gurr

1½ c. oleo	3 c. flour
3 c. sugar	2 T. lemon extract
5 eggs	¾ c. 7-Up

Cream sugar and shortening together and beat until light and fluffy. Add eggs one at a time and beat well, add flour. Beat in lemon extract and 7-Up; pour into greased bundt pan. Bake at 350°; 1½ hours.

BLUEBERRY SOUR CREAM CAKE

Edwin Watkins
In loving memory of my
Friend Sandy Adams

1 c. butter, softened   **2 c. sugar**

Slowly beating the above ingredients until light, beat in 2 eggs one at a time, fold in 1 cup sour cream and ½ teaspoon vanilla. Fold in 2 cups flour, 1 teaspoon salt, 2 teaspoons baking powder; gently fold in blueberries (fresh or frozen). Bake in a bundt pan, spray with Pam first or lightly grease. Bake at 350° for 60 minutes. Turn heat off, open oven door and allow to cool. Remove from pan when cool. Sprinkle with powdered sugar. This is my families all time summer cake.

COFFEE CAKE

Sue Stegman

5 eggs, separated

Beat egg whites until stiff.

Add to yolks:

2½ sticks oleo	**1 tsp. vanilla**
1¼ c. sugar	

Cream and beat. Add 2 cups flour; beat and fold egg whites. Grease and flour 10 x 15-inch pan. Place dough in pan and spread evenly. Plop pie filling on top. Sprinkle 1 cup powdered sugar.

SEVEN-LAYER BARS

Jean Hansel

Place the following in 9 x 13-inch pan in following order:

¼ c. butter, to grease pan	1 (6-oz.) pkg. butterscotch chips
1 c. graham cracker crumbs	1 can Eagle Brand sweetened
1 c. shredded coconut	condensed milk
1 (6-oz.) pkg. chocolate chips	1 c. chopped nuts

(continued)

Bake 30 minutes at 350°.

EASY CHOCOLATE DESSERT

Edwina Watkins

Prepare 1 (9-ounce) cake mix according to directions on package, pour into greased and floured 9 x 13-inch pan. Bake at 350° for 20 minutes. Let cool. Place softened 8-ounce package cream cheese in a large bowl and add 1 cup milk; beating constantly. Add 1 package instant chocolate pudding mix and another 1 cup milk. Beat until smooth and thickened. Spread evenly on cake and set aside. Combine 1 (8-ounce) carton whipping cream, 2 to 4 tablespoons sugar and 1/2 teaspoon vanilla. Beat until stiff peaks form. Spread over pudding layer and sprinkle almonds on top. Chill. Yields: 15 servings.

BUTTERSCOTCH SQUARES

Ruth Eisenlohr

2 c. flour	2 tsp. baking powder
1 tsp. salt	1 (12-oz.) pkg. butterscotch
1/2 c. butter or oleo	chips
2 c. firmly packed brown sugar	4 eggs
1 tsp. vanilla	1 c. nuts

Preheat oven to 350°. In small bowl combine flour, baking powder and salt. Melt over hot water, butterscotch chips, butter or oleo, remove from heat and put in large bowl. Stir in brown sugar; cool 5 minutes. Beat in eggs and vanilla. Blend in flour mixture. Stir in nuts. Spread evenly into greased 15 x 10-inch pan. Bake 30 minutes. Cut in squares.

ZUCCHINI RING

Joan Sharp

3 c. flour	1 c. oil
3 c. sugar	1/4 tsp. salt
2 tsp. baking powder	4 eggs
1 tsp. baking soda	3 c. cubed zucchini
1 1/2 tsp. cinnamon	1 c. nuts

Mix dry ingredients into large mixing bowl. Put eggs, oil and zucchini into blender. Mix until finely chopped. Add to dry ingredients. Mix with mixer until well mixed. Stir in nuts. Pour into well greased 12-cup tube pan. Bake 300°, 1 1/2 hours. Serves 12-15.

FRENCH CHERRY DESSERT

Dean Jones

½ lb. graham crackers, crushed
  (about 30 crackers or 2 c.
  crumbs)
½ c. butter or oleo, melted
2 T. sugar

2 pkgs. Dream Whip
1 c. powdered sugar
1 (8-oz.) pkg. cream cheese,
  softened
2 (1-lb.) cans cherry pie filling

Mix graham cracker crumbs, melted butter or oleo and sugar; mixing well. Reserve about ⅓ cup for garnish. Press remaining crumb mixture into 9 x 13-inch pan. Bake at 350° for 8 minutes; cool. Mix Dream Whip according to package directions. Blend cream cheese and powdered sugar together, fold into Dream Whip. Spread mixture over crumbs; top with pie filling. Sprinkle with reserved crumbs. Refrigerate overnight before serving. May be frozen for later use or stored in refrigerator for 2 to 3 days. Yields: 12 to 15 servings.

MAGGIE'S CHOCOLATE BROWNIES

Dean Jones

1 c. plus 2 T. oleo
5 squares unsweetened
  chocolate
2¼ c. sugar
5 eggs, beaten

2 tsp. vanilla
1¾ c. flour
1 tsp. salt
1½ c. chopped nuts, opt.

Melt oleo and chocolate. Add sugar, eggs and vanilla; heat thoroughly. Add flour and salt and beat until smooth. Fold in nuts. Pour into greased 9 x 13-inch pan, spread evenly. Bake 20-25 minutes in 350° oven. Cool slightly, frost if desired. Cut into 2-inch squares. Don't wait until toothpick comes out clean, they will be too done. A little mix on toothpick take out.

TEXAS FLAT CAKE

*In memory of
Elva Townsend*

2 sticks oleo
1 square chocolate
1 c. water
2 c. flour

2 c. sugar
1 tsp. baking soda
¼ tsp. salt

Bring to boil in large saucepan. Remove from heat and add:

2 eggs, slightly beaten
1 tsp. vanilla

1 c. sour milk

Pour into greased 12 x 17-inch pan. Bake 15 minutes at 400°. Mix frosting as cake bakes:

(continued)

66230-05

1 stick oleo
6 T. milk
1 square chocolate

1 lb. powdered sugar
½ c. nuts

Mix and bring to boil. Cook until blended. Frost cake while both are hot.

IMPOSSIBLE PIE

Hannah Baldwin

2 c. milk
4 eggs
½ c. sugar
1 c. coconut

1 T. vanilla
½ c. margarine
½ c. Bisquick

Blend all ingredients in the blender. Cook 350° for 30-35 minutes.

PINEAPPLE CAKE

Edwina Watkins
In loving memory of my
friend, Harriet Cobianco

Cream together with mixer:

2 c. sugar

2 eggs

Add to the first mixture:

2 c. flour
2 tsp. baking soda

½ tsp. salt

Stir in No. 2 (20-ounce) can of crushed pineapple; do not drain pineapple. Add ½ cup chopped nuts, 1 teaspoon vanilla. Can be mixed by hand or mixer. Bake in 9 x 13-inch pan, 40-45 minutes at 350°. I use a can of ready made cream cheese frosting and add some chopped nuts and top.

BROWNIE TYPE CAKE

Catherine Wildt

Boil together 2 sticks oleo, ½ cup cocoa, 1 cup water. Sift together 2 cups sugar, 2 cups flour and ¼ teaspoon salt. Pour into flour mixture the chocolate mixture and add:

2 beaten eggs
1 tsp. vanilla

1 tsp. soda
½ c. sour cream

Mix well. Bake in 9 x 13 x 1-inch pan at 400°, 20 minutes.

Frosting:

½ stick oleo
3 T. cocoa

3 T. milk

(continued)

Boil together, remove from heat and add 1 pound confectioners' sugar and 1 teaspoon vanilla. Spread on cake as soon as it is removed from oven.

DUMP CAKE

Connie Cstor

1 (1-lb. 6-oz.) can cherry pie
  filling
1 (1-lb. 4-oz.) can chunk
  pineapple

1 pkg. yellow cake mix
1 c. melted margarine
1 c. flaked coconut
1 c. walnut meats

Spread cherries over greased 13 x 9 x 2-inch baking pan. Arrange pineapple chunks over cherry filling. Sprinkle with cake mix (dry, directly from package). Cover with melted butter and top with coconut and walnuts. Bake 1 hour or until done at 350° oven.

PINEAPPLE CAKE

Inez Brimhall

2 c. sugar
2 T. oleo
2 eggs
2 c. flour
2 c. crushed pineapple, well
  drained

2 tsp. soda
1 tsp. salt
1 c. nuts

Put all ingredients in bowl and mix thoroughly. Put in greased 12 x 9-inch cake pan. Bake at 350° about 45 minutes.

Topping:

2 c. pineapple juice (add water
  to juice, drain from pineapple
  to make 2 c.)

2 T. cornstarch
2 T. butter or oleo
1 c. white sugar

Mix and bring to boil. Pour over baked cake. Allow to soak in and glaze. Serve with Cool Whip.

APPLE WALNUT CAKE

Mrs. Pumfrey

4 c. coarsely chopped apples
2 c. sugar
2 eggs
1/2 c. salad oil
2 tsp. vanilla

2 c. flour
2 tsp. baking soda
1 tsp. salt
2 tsp. cinnamon
1 c. chopped nuts

Combine apples and sugar; let stand. Beat eggs slightly, beat in oil and vanilla. Mix and add flour, baking soda, cinnamon and salt. Stir in

(continued)

alternately with apple and sugar mixture. Stir in nuts. Bake at 350° in greased and floured 13 x 9-inch pan about 1 hour.

ZUCCHINI SQUASH CAKE

Mrs. Jean Hansel

1½ c. squash, grated	2 eggs
1½ c. sugar	¾ c. oil

Mix these ingredients. Add to dry ingredients.

1¾ c. flour	½ tsp. soda
1 tsp. cinnamon	¼ tsp. salt
1 tsp. baking powder	½ c. nuts

Add ½ cup coconut last. Bake 35 minutes at 350°.

APPLESAUCE CAKE

Doris Crawford

1 c. sugar	1 tsp. soda
½ c. butter	½ tsp. baking powder
1 c. applesauce	½ tsp. cinnamon
1 egg	¼ tsp. cloves
2 c. flour	¼ tsp. allspice

Mix together and bake at 350°. Nuts, raisins, dates or coconut may be added, if desired.

PERFECT PIE CRUST

Sandy Whaley

4 c. flour	2 tsp. salt
1 T. sugar	1 egg
1¾ c. solid vegetable shortening	1 T. vinegar

Mix first 3 ingredients well. Add shortening. Beat together with fork ½ cup water, vinegar and egg. Add to dry mixture. Divide dough into 5 portions, shape into flat round patty. Wrap in plastic or waxed paper. Chill at least ½ hour. Lightly flour both sides of patty and roll out. Keeps 3 days. Yields: 2 (9-inch) double crust or 1 single crust.

NANCY'S APPLE CAKE

Nancy Cramer

1 c. sugar
2 T. shortening
1 egg
1 tsp. soda
Dash of salt

1 tsp. vanilla
1 c. sour milk
2 T. baking powder
2½ c. flour
3 c. sliced apples

Cream sugar, shortening and egg. Add vanilla and liquid with soda in it. Add flour, salt and baking powder, then apples. Place in greased and floured 9 x 13-inch pan.

Crumb Topping:

¾ c. brown sugar
2 T. butter

1 T. flour
1 tsp. cinnamon

Mix together and crumble over dough. Bake at 350° for 30-45 minutes. Good warm with ice cream.

PEANUT BUTTER FUDGE CAKE

Pauline Hoddley

1 pkg. reg. devil's food cake
  mix, non pudding
¼ c. Jif creamy peanut butter

Peanut Butter Fudge Frosting
  (recipe below)

Preheat oven to 350°. Combine cake mix with Jif. Prepare the cake mixture according to package directions. Pour batter into a greased and floured 13 x 9 x 2-inch baking pan. Bake in 350° oven, 40-45 minutes or until toothpick comes out clean. Cool. Spread with Peanut Butter Fudge Frosting.

Peanut Butter Fudge Frosting:

¼ c. Jif peanut butter
¼ c. butter or margarine,
  softened
½ tsp. vanilla

¼ c. unsweetened cocoa
  powder
6 T. hot water
2 c. confectioners' sugar

Beat Jif, butter and vanilla. Stir cocoa into hot water; add to Jif mixture. Gradually beat in sugar until of spreading consistency. Frosts 1 (13 x 9-inch) cake.

66230-05

PETER PETER PUMPKIN BARS

Donna Swagler

½ c. shortening
1 c. packed brown sugar
2 eggs
⅔ c. canned pumpkin
1 tsp. vanilla extract
1 c. all-purpose flour

1 tsp. ground cinnamon
½ tsp. baking powder
½ tsp. baking soda
¼ tsp. ground ginger
¼ tsp. ground nutmeg
½ c. chopped walnuts

Orange Frosting:

3 T. shortening
2¼ c. confectioners' sugar

3 T. orange juice
1 T. grated orange peel

Candy pumpkins

In a large mixing bowl, cream shortening and brown sugar. Add eggs, one at a time, beating well after each addition. Beat in pumpkin and vanilla. Combine the flour, cinnamon, baking powder, baking soda, ginger and nutmeg; add to creamed mixture and mix well. Stir in the nuts. Spread into a greased 13 x 9 x 2-inch baking dish. Bake at 350° for 20-25 minutes or until a toothpick inserted near the center comes out clean. Cool on a wire rack. In a mixing bowl, beat the shortening, confectioners' sugar, orange juice and orange peel until blended. Frost bars; cut into squares. Top with candy pumpkins. Preparation time: 20 minutes. Bake time: 20 minutes, plus cooling. Yields: 2 dozen.

CRAZY CAKE

Pauline Hoadley

2¼ c. flour
1½ c. sugar
4½ T. cocoa
1½ tsp. soda

¾ tsp. salt
1½ tsp. vanilla
½ c. plus 1 tsp. oil
1½ tsp. vinegar

Sift all dry ingredients into cake pan. Make 3 holes. Pour vinegar in one, vanilla in another and oil in 3rd. Pour 1½ cups water over all. Stir. Bake 30 minutes at 325°.

ORANGE PINEAPPLE DELIGHT CAKE

Pauline Hoadley

1 box yellow cake mix (or orange)
4 eggs
¾ c. oil
1 (11-oz.) can mandarin oranges & juice

1 (20-oz.) can crushed pineapple
1 sm. box vanilla pudding mix, instant
9 oz. Cool Whip

(continued)

Mix cake mix, eggs, oil and mandarin oranges and juice; pour into 9 x 13-inch greased and floured pan. Bake at 350° for 30-40 minutes. Pour ¾ cup juice from crushed pineapple over cake while still warm. Mix pineapple with pudding powder and Cool Whip. Spread over cake. Keep refrigerated.

COCONUT PINEAPPLE

Dorothy Davis Bangor

1 c. sugar
3 T. all-purpose flour
1 c. light corn syrup
1 c. flaked coconut
1 (8-oz.) can crushed pineapple,
  undrained

3 eggs, beaten
1 tsp. vanilla extract
1 (9-inch) unbaked pastry shell
¼ c. butter, melted

In a bowl, combine sugar and flour. Add the corn syrup, coconut, pineapple, eggs and vanilla; mix well. Pour into pastry shell. Drizzle with butter. Bake at 350° for 50-55 minutes or until a knife inserted near the center comes out clean. Cover loosely with foil if the top browns too quickly. Cool on a wire rack. Chill before cutting. Store in the refrigerator. Makes 6-8 servings.

SPEEDY APPLE CRISP

Dorothy Davis-Bangor

5-6 c. sliced, peeled baking
  apples
½ c. all-purpose flour
½ c. rolled oats

¾ c. packed brown sugar
½-1 tsp. ground cinnamon
⅓ c. butter or margarine

Spread apples in a 9 x 13-inch square baking pan. Combine flour, oats, sugar and cinnamon in a bowl. Cut in butter until mixture resembles coarse crumbs, sprinkle over apples. Bake at 375° for 30-35 minutes or until apples are tender and topping is golden. Serve warm. Yields: 6-8 servings.

BLUEBERRY COFFEE CAKE

Ruth Magned

½ c. butter
1 c. sugar
2 eggs
8 oz. sour cream

2 c. flour
1 tsp. baking powder
1 tsp. vanilla
2½ blueberries

Topping:

⅓ brown sugar
¼ c. sugar

½ c. nuts
1 T. melted butter

(continued)

66230-05

Put half in halfway; rest on top of batter. Bake at 325°, 40 minutes in 9 x 13-inch pan.

AUNT GLORIA'S CARROT CAKE

Mona Boone

1 c. vegetable oil	2 c. sugar
4 whole eggs	2 tsp. cinnamon
2 tsp. baking powder	2 c. flour
1 tsp. soda	1 c. chopped walnuts
1 tsp. salt	3 c. raw carrots, grated fine

Mix oil, sugar and eggs in a bowl and beat on low speed until creamy. Sift the dry ingredients together and then add a little at a time to the pervious mixture. Next, fold in nuts and carrots. Pout into 9 x 13-inch pan at 350° for 30-45 minutes. Cool in pan. Frost with Cream Cheese Frosting.

Cream Cheese Frosting:

1 (8-oz.) pkg. cream cheese	3 c. powdered sugar
½ c. margarine, softened	1 T. milk
1 tsp. vanilla	

Stir all ingredients together and beat well.

MIRACLE WHIP PINEAPPLE CAKE

Donna Swagler

Sift together:

2 c. flour	½ tsp. baking soda
1½ c. sugar	2 tsp. baking powder
1 tsp. salt	

Mix together:

1 (8-oz.) can crushed pineapple	½ tsp. lemon extract or fresh
¼ c. water	lemon
1 c. Miracle Whip	

Mix all together in greased pan; large oblong pan or big square pan. Bake at 350° till done.

FRESH APPLE CAKE

Myrna Miller

Sift together:

2½ c. flour
1½ tsp. soda
½ tsp. salt

1 tsp. cinnamon
1½ c. sugar

Stir in:

1 c. oil
2 eggs
2 tsp. vanilla

1 c. nuts
4 c. apples, cut up

Bake at 300° for 1 hour. Batter will be real thick.

PEACH COBBLER

Myrna Miller

1 c. Bisquick
1 c. sugar
⅔ c. milk

3-4 peaches
9 x 9-inch pan

Melt 1 stick of butter in pan. Pour in batter, then peaches. For 9 x 13-inch pan double recipe except for butter. Bake at 350° for 1 hour.

MOON CAKE

Myrna Miller

½ c. butter
1 c. water
1 c. flour
4 eggs
1 (8-oz.) pkg. cream cheese

1 (8-oz.) ctn. Cool Whip
Smuckers chocolate fudge
   topping for ice cream
1 lg. box instant vanilla pudding
Nuts, opt.

Bring to boil 1 cup water and butter. Add the flour at once and stir rapidly. Mixture will form a ball. Remove from heat and cool slightly. Beat in eggs one at a time. Beat well after adding each egg. Spread in a glass 9 x 13-inch baking dish that has been sprayed with Pam. Bake at 400° for 25 to 30 minutes. Cool. Mix pudding according to package directions. Mix in softened cream cheese. Spread on crust. Refrigerate 20 minutes. Top with Cool Whip. Drizzle about ½ of a 12-ounce jar of chocolate topping over the top. Add nuts, if desired.

YOGURT LEMON PIE

Mary Ann Ballard
Leesburg, FL

1/3 c. milk
1 (8-oz.) pkg. cream cheese,
  softened
2 c. plain yogurt
1 (3.4-oz.) pkg. instant lemon
  pudding mix

1 (9-inch) graham cracker crust
Whipped topping, opt.
Lemon peel, cut into very thin
  strips, opt.

In a mixing bowl, beat milk and cream cheese until smooth. Stir in yogurt until smooth. Add pudding mix and blend until mixture begins to thicken. Spoon into crust. Refrigerate until serving time. If desired, garnish with whipped topping and lemon strips.

EASY SOUTHERN BANANA PUDDING

Elva Fisher

3 c. cold fat-free milk
Wafers (30 reduced-fat Nilla)
2 (4-oz.) pkgs. vanilla instant
  pudding

3 bananas, sliced
3 c. thawed Cool Whip, lite

Pour milk into large bowl. Add dry pudding mixes. Beat with wire whisk 2 minutes or until well blended. Let stand 5 minutes. Arrange half of wafers on bottom and up sides of a 2-quart serving bowl. Add layers of half each bananas and pudding. Repeat layers. Spread Cool Whip over pudding. Refrigerate 3 hours or until ready to serve.

LEMON BARS

Pauline Hoadley

Crust:

1 c. all-purpose flour
1/3 c. butter, softened

1/4 c. confectioners' sugar

Topping:

1 c. sugar
2 eggs
2 T. all-purpose flour
2 T. lemon juice

1/2 tsp. lemon extract
1/2 tsp. baking powder
1/4 tsp. salt
Confectioners' sugar

Combine the crust ingredients and pat into a 8-inch square baking pan. Bake at 375° for 15 minutes. Meanwhile, for topping, combine the sugar, eggs, flour, lemon juice, extract, baking powder and salt in a mixing bowl. Mix until frothy; pour over crust. Bake at 375° for 18-22 minutes or until light golden brown. Dust with confectioners' sugar. Yields: 9 servings.

TONI KISEL'S APPLE CAKE

Pauline Hoadley

4 c. diced apples   2 c. sugar

Mix apples and sugar and let stand.

2 c. flour   2 tsp. vanilla
1½ tsp. soda   ⅔ c. oil
1 tsp. salt   2 eggs
1 tsp. cinnamon   1 c. chopped nuts

Beat eggs, oil and vanilla. Add dry ingredients. Mix well. Batter will be stiff. Blend in apple/sugar mixture. Stir in nuts. Raisins may be used in place of nuts. Bake in greased 9 x 13-inch pan at 350° for 45 minutes.

FRUIT COCKTAIL CAKE

Madeline Cramer

1½ c. sugar   1 tsp. soda
2¼ c. flour   1 (1-lb. 1-oz.) can fruit cocktail
¼ tsp. salt   2 eggs

Stir above ingredients together, pour in 9 x 13-inch pan. Sprinkle with powdered sugar, coconut and nuts. Bake 325° oven for 40 minutes.

1 c. powdered sugar   1 c. coconut
1 c. nuts, walnuts or pecans

Cover with sauce made of (after baked).

¾ c. sugar   ½ c. evaporated milk
1 stick oleo

Cook for 3 minutes, add 1 teaspoon vanilla.

LEMON-CRANBERRY BARS

Pauline Hoadley

½ c. frozen lemonade   1½ c. all-purpose flour
  concentrate, thawed   2 tsp. grated lemon peel
½ c. spoonable sugar substitute   ½ tsp. baking soda
¼ c. margarine   ½ tsp. salt
1 egg   ½ c. dried cranberries

Preheat oven to 375°. Lightly coat 8-inch square baking pan with non-stick cooking spray; set aside. Combine lemonade concentrate, sugar substitute, margarine and egg in medium bowl; mix well. Add flour, lemon peel, baking soda and salt; stir well. Stir in cranberries; spoon into prepared pan. Bake 20 minutes or until light brown. Cool completely in pan on wire rack. Cut into 16 squares.

PEANUT BUTTER CHOCOLATE BARS

Pauline Hoadley

1 c. Equal spoonful*
½ c. (1 stick) butter or
  margarine, softened
⅓ c. firmly packed brown sugar
½ c. 2% milk
½ c. creamy peanut butter
1 egg

1 tsp. vanilla
1 c. all-purpose flour
¾ c. quick oats, uncooked
½ tsp. baking soda
¼ tsp. salt
¾ c. mini semi-sweet chocolate
  chips

*May substitute 24 packets Equal sweetener. Beat Equal, butter and brown sugar until well combined. Stir in milk, peanut butter, egg and vanilla until blended. Gradually mix in combined flour, oats, baking soda and salt until blended. Stir in chocolate chips. Spread mixture evenly in 9 x 13-inch pan generously coated with non-stick cooking spray. Bake in preheated 350° oven 20 to 22 minutes. Cool completely in pan on wire rack. Cut into squares; store in airtight container at room temperature. Makes 48 bars.

KIM'S EASY DESSERT

Kim Rhoads

1 can sweetened condensed
  milk
1 pkg. Kool-Aid, any flavor

1 reg. ctn. Cool Whip
1 graham cracker crust

Mix milk, Kool-Aid, add ½ container of Cool Whip.

INSTANT RICE PUDDING

Londa Wines

1 c. instant rice
2½ c. milk, divided
¼ tsp. salt
¼ tsp. cinnamon
⅛ tsp. nutmeg

½ c. sugar
¼ c. raisins
2 eggs, slightly beaten
½ tsp. vanilla

Combine rice, 2 cups milk, salt, cinnamon, nutmeg, sugar and raisins. Bring to a rolling boil, stirring constantly. Reduce heat and boil slowly 10 minutes stirring occasionally. Mix eggs with remaining milk. Slowly add to hot mixture, stirring constantly. Cook over medium heat until thickened. Add vanilla. Let cool 10 minutes. Makes 6 servings.

BLUEBERRY MUFFINS

Londa Wines

1 egg	½ c. sugar
½ c. milk	2 tsp. baking powder
¼ c. cooking oil	½ tsp. salt
1½ c. flour	1 c. blueberries, fresh or frozen

Preheat oven to 400°. Beat slightly with fork egg, milk and oil. In small bowl combine flour, sugar, baking powder and salt. Add to wet ingredients; stir until moistened. Batter should be lumpy. Do not over mix. Fill muffin cups ⅔ full. Baking time: 20-25 minutes. Will make 12 medium muffins.

FRUIT MAGIC

Londa Wines

1 (1-lb. 5-oz.) can cherry pie filling	¼ c. margarine
1 pkg. Jiffy cake mix	½ c. chopped nuts

Preheat oven to 350°. Spread pie filling in 8 x 8-inch square pan. Combine cake mix and nuts in bowl. Add soft margarine and mix until crumbly. Sprinkle over top of pie filling. Bake 45 to 50 minutes until golden brown. Good served warm with ice cream or Cool Whip. Yields: 6 servings.

SOUR CREAM PUMPKIN COFFEE CAKE HOMEMADE WITH LOVE

½ c. butter	1 c. sour cream
¾ c. sugar	1¾ c. (16-oz. can) Libby's solid pack pumpkin
1 tsp. vanilla	
3 eggs	1 slightly beaten egg
2 c. flour	⅓ c. sugar
1 tsp. baking powder	1 tsp. pumpkin pie spice
1 tsp. baking soda	Streusel

Cream butter, ¾ cup sugar and vanilla in mixer bowl. Add 3 eggs beating well. Combine flour, baking powder and baking soda. Add dry ingredients to butter mixture alternately with sour cream. Combine pumpkin, beaten egg, ⅓ cup sugar and pie spice. Spoon half of batter into 13 x 9 x 2-inch baking dish; spread to corners. Sprinkle half of Streusel over batter. Spread pumpkin mixture over Streusel. Carefully spread remaining batter over pumpkin mixture. Sprinkle remaining Streusel over top. Bake in slow oven (325°) 50-60 minutes or until toothpick inserted in center comes out clean. **Streusel:** Cut 1 cup firmly

(continued)

packed brown sugar, ⅓ cup butter and 2 teaspoons cinnamon together until blended. Stir in 1 cup chopped nuts. Makes 12 servings.

BIBLE CAKE

Luella Pumfrey

4½ c. 1 Kings 4:22
1 pinch Lev. 2:13
Season to taste 11 Chron. 9:9
1½ c. Judg. 5:25, last clause
2 c. Jer. 6:20

6 Jer. 17:11
2 T. 1 Sam. 30:12
2 c. Nahum 3:12
1 c. Num. 17:8
½ c. Judg. 4:19, last clause

Mix all together and add 2 teaspoons Amos 4:5. Finish with Exodus 16:23.

PINA COLADA CAKE

Marilyn Clayton

1 box Duncan Hines white cake
  mix
¼ c. oil
1⅓ c. water

2 eggs, beaten
1 lg. can coconut
1 (15-oz.) can cream of coconut
1 (12 to 16 oz.) Cool Whip

In 13 x 9 x 2-inch pan, put in oil and make sure sides are covered with oil. Add cake mix, water, eggs and ½ of coconut. Mix until lumpy and runny. Put in oven and bake 30-35 minutes at 350°. Take knife and indent holes in top of cake and pour cream of coconut over cake. Put cake in fridge to cool. Take rest of coconut (½ package); mix into Cool Whip and cover top of cake. Pineapple can be added to cake or icing.

CHERRIES IN THE SNOW

Tony Kisel

Mix together: One and ½ cup graham cracker crumbs and ¼ cup melted margarine and spread in bottom of pan. Whip 1 envelope Dream Whip, 1 package cream cheese, 1 cup marshmallows, ½ cup sugar and 1 teaspoon vanilla. Mix together and fold into Dream Whip mixture. Spread in pan; pour 1 cup cherry filling over top. Refrigerate several hours. Any fruit can be used.

QUICK JELLO DESSERT

Pearl Sarno

1 bowl Cool Whip
1 can mandarin oranges

1 lb. cottage cheese
1 can pineapple tidbits

(continued)

Mix together and add 1 package dry Jello (orange). Any flavor Jello may be used. An entirely different dessert can be made by varying the color Jello and the kind of fruit added. Mix well, garnish with cherries & nuts, if desired.

HEAVENLY DELIGHT

Hannah Baldwin

Two cups vanilla wafers, crushed and 2 tablespoons butter in 9 x 13-inch pan.

¾ c. margarine	2 eggs
1 c. powdered sugar	

Put in blender and mix.

1 c. crushed pineapple, drained, save juice	1 c. whipped cream
1 c. pecans or walnuts	Wafer crumbs & juice

Six layers. Cover and refrigerate overnight.

BLUEBERRY BUCKLE

MaryAnn Ballard
Leesburg, FL

¼ c. shortening	½ tsp. salt
½ c. sugar	½ c. milk
1 egg	2½ c. fresh or frozen
1 c. all-purpose flour	blueberries
1½ tsp. baking powder	

Topping:

¼ c. butter	⅓ c. all-purpose flour
½ c. sugar	½ tsp. ground cinnamon

In a medium mixing bowl, cream shortening and sugar. Beat in egg. Combine flour, baking powder and salt; add alternately with milk to creamed mixture. Pour into an ungreased 8-inch square baking pan. Arrange blueberries on top. In another mixing bowl, cream butter and sugar. Combine flour and cinnamon; add gradually to creamed mixture. Crumble over blueberries. Bake at 350° for 45-50 minutes.

CHERRY CRUNCH OR OTHER FRUIT

Hazel Cramer

½ c. butter (1 stick)	1 (9-oz.) pkg. cake mix
1 can cherry pie filling	½ c. chopped nut meats

(continued)

Grease 8 x 8 x 2-inch cake pan. Pour in pie filling. Cover with dry cake mix. Sprinkle melted butter on top then nut meats. Bake 35-45 minutes in 350° oven.

WHIP CREAM FROSTING

Sandy Whaley

Cook 1 cup milk and ¼ cup flour until thick. Cool until cold. Mix together ¾ cup shortening and 1 cup sugar. Beat in flour and milk; add 1 teaspoon vanilla.

NO COOK FROSTING

Sandy Whaley

2 egg whites
¼ tsp. salt
¼ c. sugar

¾ c. Karo light syrup
1¼ tsp. vanilla

Beat egg whites and salt; beat in sugar. Beat until smooth and glossy. Beat in syrup and vanilla.

BLUEBERRY STREUSEL COFFEE CAKE

Londa Wines

3 c. flour
1 c. sugar
3 tsp. baking powder
½ tsp. salt
2 eggs, beaten
½ c. milk

½ c. softened margarine
¾ c. sour cream
1½ c. blueberries, fresh or
   frozen
½ c. pecan pieces, opt.

With mixer cream sugar and margarine, add eggs, mix, then add sour cream and milk using mixer. Mix in flour, baking powder and salt. Add blueberries and pecans (optional). Grease or spray a 9 x 13-inch cake pan. Preheated oven 375° about 40 minutes. Check with toothpick.

Streusel Topping:

⅓ c. white sugar
⅓ c. brown sugar
⅓ c. flour

¼ c. cold margarine
¼ tsp. cinnamon
A few nuts, opt.

Cut cold margarine up with sugars and cinnamon. Serve with Cool Whip, if desired.

STRAWBERRY RHUBARB CRUNCH

Donna Swagler

2 c. frozen rhubarb, drain
  juice & throw away
2 c. frozen strawberries, thaw
  slightly
1/2 c. sugar
1/2 c. softened butter

1/4 tsp. apple pie spice or
  cinnamon
1/2 c. nuts, if wanted
1 c. oatmeal
3/4 c. firmly packed brown sugar
1 c. flour

Combine in bowl rhubarb, strawberries, granulated sugar. If out of strawberries use strawberry jam. Put in 8 x 8-inch baking pan. In separate
bowl, mix brown sugar, flour, oatmeal together and add softened butter.
Spread over rhubarb and bake in microwave until bubbly about 11
minutes. If using fresh rhubarb add some tapioca or flour for thicker.

FRESH STRAWBERRY PIE

Edwina Watkins

1 c. water
3/4 c. sugar
2 T. cornstarch
1 sm. pkg. strawberry Jello

1 (8- or 9-inch) graham cracker
  crust
Cool Whip
1 qt. fresh strawberries

Cut the strawberries into halves and place into layers in the graham
cracker crust, place all strawberries with cut side down. Cook water,
sugar and cornstarch until thick in medium saucepan. Pour Jello into
thickened mixture. Stir well. Pour over strawberries in pie crust. Chill
and serve with Cool Whip.

AMAZING COCONUT PIE

Pat Jones

2 c. milk
1/2 c. biscuit mix or self-rising
  flour
3/4 c. sugar

4 eggs
1/4 c. margarine
1 1/2 tsp. vanilla flavoring
1 c. coconut

Preheat oven to 350°. Combine all ingredients except coconut in blender
and blend on low speed 3 minutes. Pour in greased 9-inch pie pan. Let
stand 5 minutes and then sprinkle with coconut. Bake 40 minutes.

UGLY DUCKLING CAKE

Dorothy Davis Bangor

1 pkg. yellow cake mix
1 (16-oz.) can fruit cocktail
2 1/2 c. coconut, flaked
2 eggs

1/2 c. firmly packed brown sugar
1/2 c. butter or margarine
1/2 c. sugar
1/2 c. evaporated milk

(continued)

66230-05

Combine cake mix, fruit cocktail with syrup, 1 cup of the coconut and the eggs in large mixer bowl. Blend, then beat at medium speed for 2 minutes. Pour into 9 x 13-inch pan. Sprinkle with brown sugar. Bake at 325° for 45 minutes or until cake springs back when lightly touched. Bring butter, sugar and milk to a boil; boil 2 minutes. Remove from heat, stir in remaining coconut, spoon over hot cake in pan. Serve warm or cool.

BLUEBERRY CREAM CHEESE PIE

Edwina Watkins

Crust, no rolling
1½ c. flour
½ tsp. salt

2 T. sugar
½ c. vegetable oil
2 T. milk

Mix ingredients together and press into an 8- or 9-inch pie pan, flute edges. Prick crust with fork and bake 375° for 15 minutes or until lightly brown. When cool, spread 8 ounces cream cheese softened with the milk onto crust.

Filling:

1 c. sugar
2 T. plus 2 tsp. cornstarch
⅛ tsp. salt
1 c. water

4 c. fresh or frozen blueberries, divided
1 T. butter
1 T. lemon juice

Mix sugar, cornstarch and salt, add water and 2 cups blueberries; cook and stir until thick. Add butter, 2 cups blueberries and lemon juice. Cool. Pour into baked crust and chill. Top with Cool Whip and decorate with blueberries.

FRUIT CRUMB PIE BARS

Dorothy Davis Bangor

3 c. all-purpose flour
1 c. sugar
½ tsp. baking soda
½ lb. butter or margarine, melted

1 can pie filling (apple, blueberry, cherry or peach)

Sift dry ingredients together into a large bowl. Pour melted butter or margarine into dry ingredients and mix well by hand. Reserve 1 cup of mixture for topping. Press remaining mixture into cookie sheet with lip. Spread can of pie filling evenly over top and then sprinkle reserved crumbs on top of filling. Bake 350° for 45 minutes to 1 hour until light brown on top. While warm, cut into 2 (1-inch) squares. Makes 2 dozen bars.

Recipe Favorites

COOKIES
& CANDY

*Taste and see that the
Lord is good; blessed is the
man who takes refuge in him.*

~ Psalm 34:8

Helpful Hints

- Push animal shaped cookie cutters lightly into icing on cakes or cupcakes. Fill depressed outlines with chocolate icing or decorating confections.

- Fill flat bottomed ice cream cones half full with cake batter and bake. Top with icing and decorating confections.

- To make cookie crumbs for your recipes, put cookies into a plastic bag and run a rolling pin back and forth until they are the right size.

- To decorate cookies with chocolate, place cookies on a rack over waxed paper. Dip the tines of a fork with chocolate, and wave the fork gently back and forth making wavy lines.

- A gadget that works well for decorating sugar cookies is an empty plastic thread spool. Simply press the spool into the dough, imprinting a pretty flower design.

- Some holiday cookies require an indent on top to fill with jam or chocolate. Use the rounded end of a honey dipper to make the indent.

- Tin coffee cans make excellent freezer containers for cookies.

- If you only have one cookie sheet on hand, line it with parchment paper. While one batch is baking, load a second sheet of parchment paper to have another batch ready to bake. Cleaning is also easier.

- When a recipe calls for packed brown sugar, fill the correct size measuring cup with the sugar, and then use the next smaller size cup to pack the brown sugar into its cup.

- Dipping strawberries in chocolate? Stick toothpicks into the stem end of the berry. Coat the berries with chocolate, shaking off any excess. Turn the berries upside down and stick the toothpick into a block of styrofoam until the chocolate is set. The finished berries will have chocolate with no flat spots. Another easy solution is to place dipped berries dipped-side up in the holes of an egg carton.

- Cut-up dried fruit sometimes sticks to the blade of your knife. To prevent this problem, coat the blade of your knife with a thin film of vegetable spray before cutting.

- Cutting dessert bars is easier if you score the bars as soon as the pan comes out of the oven. When the bars cool, cut along the scored lines.

COOKIES & CANDY

COWBOY COOKIES

Pauline Hoadley

Cream:

2-1 c. shortening or margarine
2-1 c. white sugar
4-2 eggs

2-1 c. brown sugar
2-1 tsp. vanilla

Add:

4-2 c. flour
1-½ tsp. baking powder

2-1 tsp. soda
1-½ tsp. salt

Mix in:

4-2 c. oatmeal
½ pkg. (12-oz.) chocolate chips,
  I use less

1 c. chopped nuts, opt.

Bake at 350° for 10-12 minutes.

CHOCOLATE CHIP COOKIES

Ruth Magner

1 c. Smart Balance
½ c. brown sugar

½ c. Splenda
2 eggs

1 tsp. vanilla
1½ c. flour

1 tsp. baking powder
1 c. quick oats

1 c. sweet cranberries, chopped
½ c. chopped walnuts
½ c. flake coconut

1 pkg. semi-sweet chocolate
  chunks

Chill dough overnight. Bake at 375° for 10-12 minutes.

MOLASSES OAT COOKIE

Lill Gurr

1 c. sugar
½ c. molasses
1 c. shortening
2 eggs
2 c. rolled oats
1 tsp. cloves

½ tsp. soda
2 c. flour
1 c. chopped raisins
½ c. milk
2 tsp. cinnamon
½ c. butternuts

Mix ingredients in order given. Melt the shortening before adding. Sift soda and spices with flour. Drop by teaspoon on greased pan and bake at 375° for 10 minutes.

COOKIES

1 c. dates, chopped fine
1 c. Eagle Brand milk

1 c. nuts, chopped fine
Box Ritz crackers

Heat the first three ingredients in a double boiler, mixing well until warm and thick. Put a spoonful on each cracker. Bake at 325° for 8 to 10 minutes or until slightly brown. Cool a little. Frost with a thin powdered sugar frosting. Makes about 50.

CREAM CHEESE COOKIES

Pearl Sarno

½ c. packed brown sugar
1 c. Bisquick
1 (8-oz.) pkg. cream cheese
1 T. lemon juice
½ tsp. vanilla

¼ c. oleo or butter
½ c. chopped walnuts
¼ c. granulated sugar
2 tsp. milk
1 egg

Heat oven to 350°. Grease 8 x 8 x 2-inch square pan. Beat brown sugar and oleo until fluffy. Stir in baking mix and walnuts until mixture is crumbly; reserve 1 cup. Press remaining mixture in pan. Bake 12 minutes. Mix cream cheese and granulated sugar, beat in rest of ingredients until smooth. Spread cheese mixture over layer in pan; sprinkle with reserved crumbly mixture. Bank until center is firm, about 25 minutes. Cut into 2-inch squares. Store cookies in refrigerator. Makes 16 cookies.

WALNUT BUTTER COOKIES

Irene Blakemore

¼ c. butter or margarine
⅓ c. granulated sugar
1 egg
¾ tsp. soda
⅓ c. chopped walnuts

¼ c. shortening
⅓ c. brown sugar
1⅓ c. flour
1 tsp. vanilla

Melt shortening, add sugars. Mix well, add egg. Beat till light colored, add flour and soda into egg mixture. Add vanilla and nuts. Chill. Roll in small balls or drop from teaspoon onto cookie sheet, ungreased. Bake in moderate oven 375°, 7 to 10 minutes.

HOLIDAY FRUIT DROPS

Luella Pumfrey

Cream 1 cup shortening, 2 cups brown sugar. Beat in 2 eggs. Stir in ½ cup sour milk or buttermilk. Sift together 3½ cups sifted flour, 1

(continued)

66230-05

teaspoon soda, 1 teaspoon salt. Add dry ingredients to butter mixture. Add ½ cup chopped nuts, 2 cups candied cherries (halved) and 2 cups raisins or date pieces. Chill 1 hour. Bake on lightly greased sheets 15 minutes at 150°.

CHRISTMAS CANDY

Maude Moore

1 stick oleo   **1 (6-oz.) pkg. chocolate chips**

Melt together. Add 1¼ cups powdered sugar, 1 egg, ¾ cup chopped nut meats and ½ package colored miniature marshmallows. Mix all ingredients, using 2 pieces of wax paper. Divide mixture into 2 parts, shape in long rolls. Work marshmallows in. Take fresh wax paper and spread with coconut or chopped nuts. Roll and refrigerate. Slice when thoroughly chilled.

PEANUT BUTTER BON BONS

Ruth Eisenholr

1 c. nuts   **1 c. dates**
1 c. powdered sugar   **1 c. peanut butter**

Roll in balls after thoroughly blended. Stand for couple of days. Then dip in paraffin and chocolate mixture.

BON-BON CANDY

Ruth Eisenlohr

1 c. peanut butter   **1 c. nuts, chopped**
1 c. powdered sugar   **1 c. dates, cut into small pieces**

Mix and make into balls. Then set, dip them in melted chocolate.

MARTHA WASHINGTON CANDY

Marilyn Clayton

1 lb. soft oleo   **1 lg. pkg. fine pecans**
1 lg. pkg. coconut   **1½ lg. pkg. chocolate chips**
3½ lbs. powdered sugar   **½ cake of paraffin**
1 T. vanilla

Mix well the oleo, coconut, powdered sugar, vanilla and pecans; form into balls; roll in powdered sugar. Melt chocolate chips and paraffin. Lift balls with toothpick and dip in chocolate. Place on cookie sheet and refrigerate. Makes 165 balls.

VELVEETA FUDGE

Dean Jones

2 lbs. powdered sugar
½ c. cocoa
2 sticks oleo

8-oz. pkg. Velveeta cheese
Nuts, if desired

Melt oleo and cheese in saucepan. Mix powdered sugar and cocoa in large bowl. We use Tupperware green bowl. Add nuts. When completely melted, stir the oleo and cheese mixture into the sugar-cocoa mixture. Pat into ungreased cookie sheet or size pan for desired thickness. Let cool. Eat.

CRACKER JACK

Connie Castor

2 c. brown sugar
½ c. Karo
1 tsp. soda

2 sticks oleo
1 tsp. salt
1 tsp. buttered seasoning

Cook 5 minutes. It does not have to boil. Pour over 6 cups popcorn (nuts can be added, if desired). Spread on cookie sheets and bake 1 hour at 200°.

PEANUT BRITTLE

Connie Castor

1 c. white sugar
1 c. white Karo

2 c. raw peanuts

Cook till temperature on candy thermometer reaches 360°. Add 1 tablespoon soda. Stir until well mixed and color changes light caramel color and pour onto a greased cookie sheet. Let cool and break into pieces.

QUICK COOKIES-NO BAKE

Helen Peterson

Put in a pan large enough to boil: ½ cup milk, 2 cups sugar, ¾ stick oleo and 4 tablespoons cocoa. Boil 1 minute. Remove from heat and add: ½ cup peanut butter, 1 tablespoon vanilla, 2 cups oatmeal, 1 cup nuts and 1 cup coconut. Drop by teaspoonful on wax paper. Let cool.

66230-05

CHOCOLATE GLAZED OATMEAL BARS

Virginia Kenney

½ c. flour	¾ c. chocolate chips
½ tsp. baking soda	½ tsp. salt
¾ c. packed brown sugar	½ c. butter or oleo, softened
1 tsp. vanilla	1 egg
¾ c. finely chopped walnuts	1½ c. quick Quaker oats

Stir together flour, salt and soda; set aside. In large bowl cream butter, sugar, egg and vanilla until fluffy. Stir in flour mixture, oatmeal and 1 cup nuts. Spread mixture evenly in well greased 13 x 9 x 2-inch pan. Bake in preheated 375° oven, 12 minutes or until golden brown and firm to touch. Remove pan to rack, sprinkle evenly with chocolate pieces. Let stand until chocolate melts, spread evenly and sprinkle with remaining nuts. Cool until chocolate hardens and cut with sharp knife. Makes 36 bars.

BLACK WALNUT WAFERS

Helen Peterson

Beat 2 eggs until light, add 1 cup firmly packed light brown sugar and beat until thick. Add ⅔ cup flour, ½ teaspoon each of salt and baking powder. Add 1 cup finely chopped black walnuts. Drop by scant teaspoon onto greased cookie sheet. Bake in 400° oven for 5 minutes. Let stand for ½ minute before removing. Makes 5 dozen.

FORGOTTEN COOKIES

Ruth Eisenlohr

2 egg whites, beaten stiff

Add:

¾ c. sugar, gradually

Fold in:

**½ c. chopped nuts or ½ c.
chopped dates or ½ c.
chocolate chips**

Preheat oven to 350°. Drop cookies on well buttered cookie sheet. Put in oven and turn off heat. Leave in overnight or several hours.

PINEAPPLE COOKIES

Pauline Hoadley

1 c. shortening
1½ c. sugar
1 egg
1 (8¾-oz.) can crushed
  pineapple with juice

3½ c. flour
1 tsp. soda
½ tsp. salt
¼ tsp. nutmeg
½ c. chopped nuts

Mix and chill at least an hour. Bake at 400°, 8-10 minutes on lightly greased cookie sheet.

RED & GREEN COOKIES

Connie Castor

½ c. butter, softened
1 c. light brown sugar
1 tsp. vanilla
2 c. chopped pecans
½ lb. candied red cherries

1 c. flour
2 eggs
Pinch salt
6 slices candied pineapple

Preheat oven to 300°. In large bowl, with electric mixer at high speed, beat butter with sugar until fluffy. Add eggs and beat until light. Add vanilla and salt. At low speed, beat in flour. Grease and flour 2 (11 x 7 x 2-inch) pans. Sprinkle 1 cup nuts in each pan. Drop batter on nuts; spread evenly over nuts. Press the candied pineapple and cherries into batter. Bake 30 to 40 minutes or until golden brown. Cut into squares while warm. Makes 4 dozen.

CREAM CHEESE COOKIES

Pauline Hoadley

1 c. butter
1 (3-oz.) cream cheese
1 c. sugar

2½ c. flour
1 egg yolk
1 tsp. vanilla

Mix, drop by teaspoon, flatten with fork. Bake at 325°-350°, 10-13 minutes.

BROWNIES

Pauline Chernoff

1 c. butter
2 c. sugar
4 eggs
1 tsp. vanilla

2 c. flour
3 squares chocolate, melted
1 c. nut meats, cut up

(continued)

60

Cream butter and sugar, add whole eggs, one at a time and beat well. Add flour, chocolate and nuts. Spread in greased pan. Bake 30 minutes at 300°. While still warm cut in squares.

CHEESE DANISH

Pauline Hoadley

2 pkgs. crescent rolls
1 egg
1 c. sugar

2 (8-oz.) pkgs. cream cheese
1 tsp. vanilla

Unroll and lay 1 package crescent rolls in bottom of 9 x 13-inch dish. Beat cream cheese, egg, sugar and vanilla and pour on crescent rolls in pan. Lay another pack of rolls on top of cream cheese mixture and bake in 350° oven for 30 minutes. Cool and drizzle with powdered sugar frosting.

ROCKY ROAD FUDGE BARS

½ c. butter or margarine
1 sq. unsweetened chocolate or
  1 env. pre-melted
1 c. sugar
1 c. flour

½ to 1 c. nuts
1 tsp. baking powder
1 tsp. vanilla
2 eggs

Filling:

8-oz. pkg. cream cheese,
  reserve 2 oz. for frosting
½ c. sugar
2 T. flour
¼ c. butter or margarine

1 egg
½ tsp. vanilla
¼ c. chopped nuts
6-oz. pkg. (1 c.) semi-sweet
  chocolate pieces, if desired

Frosting:

2 c. miniature marshmallows
¼ c. butter or margarine
1 sq. unsweetened chocolate
Remaining 2 oz. cream cheese

¼ c. milk
3 c. powdered sugar
1 tsp. vanilla

Preheat oven to 350°. Grease (no oil) and flour 13 x 9-inch pan. In large saucepan over low heat, melt ½ cup butter and 1 ounce chocolate. Lightly spoon flour into measuring cup; level off. Add remaining bar ingredients; mix well. Spread in prepared pan. In small bowl, combine 6 ounces cream cheese with next 5 filling ingredients. Beat 1 minute at medium speed until smooth and fluffy; stir in nuts. Spread over chocolate mixture. Sprinkle with chocolate pieces. Bake 25 to 35 minutes until toothpick inserted in center comes out clean. Remove from oven; sprinkle with marshmallows. Bake 2 minutes longer. Meanwhile in large saucepan, over low heat, melt ¼ cup butter, 1 square chocolate,

(continued)

remaining 2 ounces cream cheese and milk. Stir in powdered sugar and vanilla until smooth. Immediately pour over marshmallows and swirl together. Cool; cut into bars. Store in refrigerator. Yields: 3 to 4 dozen bars.

BOHEMIAN COOKIES

Ruth Eisenlohr

1 c. oleo or butter
1¼ c. powdered sugar
6 oz. sweet chocolate, ground
1 c. nuts, ground

Dash of salt
1¼ c. sifted flour
1 tsp. vanilla

Cream shortening, add sugar and cream together until fluffy. Add remaining ingredients and mix well. Drop by teaspoon on ungreased cookie sheet. Bake at 250° oven for 40 minutes. Makes 5 dozen.

PEANUT BUTTER CANDY-COOKIES

Irene Blackmore

½ c. packed brown sugar
¼ c. evaporated milk

½ c. peanut butter
2½ c. Rice Krispies

Put first 3 ingredients in saucepan and bring to boiling. Stir constantly until sugar is dissolved and peanut butter is melted. Remove from fire. Stir in Rice Krispies. Drop by teaspoon onto wax paper. Makes 3 dozen.

YUM YUM SQUARES

Tony Kisel

⅔ c. margarine, melted & cooled
1 lb. brown sugar
3 eggs
1 tsp. each vanilla and water

2½ c. flour
2½ tsp. baking powder
1 tsp. salt
1 (6-oz.) pkg. chocolate chips
1 c. broken walnuts

Beat margarine, sugar, eggs, vanilla and water with electric mixer until blended. Add sifted dry ingredients, chocolate pieces and walnuts and mix thoroughly. Spread in a greased and floured 15½ x 10½ x 1-inch jelly-roll pan. Bake at 350° for 25 minutes.

NUTMEG LOGS

Lill Gurr

Cream together 1 cup butter or margarine, 2 teaspoons vanilla and 2 teaspoons rum flavoring. Gradually add ¾ cup sugar, cream well and

(continued)

blend in 1 egg. Add sifted 3 cups flour and 1 teaspoon nutmeg gradually into creamed mixture. Shape pieces of dough into long rolls ½-inch diameter. Cut into 3-inch lengths. Bake on ungreased cookie sheet in 350° oven 12 to 15 minutes until light golden brown. Cool, spread with frosting. Mark with tines of fork. Decorate with sprinkles.

Frosting:

3 T. butter
½ tsp. vanilla
1 tsp. rum flavoring

2½ c. sifted confectioners' sugar
2-3 T. cream or milk

WALNUT COOKIES

Irene Blakemore

½ c. shortening
⅓ c. sugar
⅓ c. brown sugar
⅓ c. chopped nuts

1⅓ c. flour
1 tsp. vanilla
1 egg

Melt shortening, add sugars, soda and egg, then flour. Mix and add vanilla and nuts. Drop from teaspoon. Bake on cookie sheet at 375°, 7-10 minutes.

GREEN TOMATO MINCEMEAT BUTTERSCOTCH COOKIES

½ c. shortening
2 c. brown sugar
2 well-beaten eggs
1 tsp. vanilla

3½ c. flour
½ tsp. salt
1 tsp. soda
1 tsp. cream of tartar

Thoroughly cream shortening and sugar; add eggs and vanilla. Add sifted dry ingredients; mix well. Form into roll, 1½ inch in diameter; wrap in waxed paper and chill thoroughly or overnight. Slice and arrange half the slices on greased cookie sheet. Place 1 teaspoon filling on each and top with remaining slices; make a cross shape steam hole on top. Press edges together with fingers or fork. Bake in moderate oven 350° for 10 minutes or longer. Makes 5 dozen. Taken from date filled recipe from Betty Crocker Cookbook. Dorothy makes balls and flattens with glass. Evelyn rolls her dough out and uses 2-inch glass to cut out and does not chill dough. Also a 2-inch cookie is easier to work with.

MINCEMEAT COOKIES

Toni Kisel

1 c. shortening	3¼ c. sifted flour
1¼ c. sugar	½ tsp. salt
3 eggs, slightly beaten	1 tsp. soda
1½ c. ready to use mincemeat	

Cream together shortening and sugar until light and fluffy. Add eggs and beat until smooth. Stir in mincemeat. Sift together flour, salt and soda. Add to shortening mixture and mix thoroughly. Drop from teaspoon onto greased baking sheet, about 2 inches apart. Bake 375° about 12 minutes or until golden brown. Makes 6 dozen.

RAISIN COCONUT BARS

½ c. oleo	¼ tsp. salt
1 c. brown sugar	½ tsp. vanilla
1 egg, beaten	¾ c. seedless raisins
⅔ c. flour, sifted	⅓ c. shredded coconut
½ tsp. baking powder	

Melt oleo and blend in sugar. Add egg and beat thoroughly. Sift together flour, baking powder and salt. Stir into first mixture. Blend in vanilla and raisins and mix well. Spread in a greased 8-inch square pan. Sprinkle with coconut. Bake 350°, 30 minutes. Cool and cut into bars. Makes 2 dozen bars.

OATMEAL PINEAPPLE COOKIES

Virginia Kenny

1 can crushed pineapple in syrup	2 c. flour
1½ c. packed brown sugar	1 tsp. baking powder
1 c. butter or oleo, softened	1 tsp. salt
1 egg	1 tsp. cinnamon
¼ tsp. almond extract	½ tsp. nutmeg
4 c. oatmeal, uncooked	¾ oz. slivered almonds
	2 c. flaked coconut

Drain pineapple well. Reserve ½ cup syrup. Cream sugar and butter until light and fluffy. Beat in egg. Beat in pineapple, reserved syrup and extract. Combine oats, flour, baking powder, salt and spices; stir into mixture, add almonds, coconut. If desired a package of chocolate chips may be added. Drop on greased cookie sheet. Bake 350° for 20 to 25 minutes until golden. Cool on wire racks. Makes 4½ to 5 dozen cookies.

66230-05

FRUIT CAKE COOKIES

Maude Merrill

½ c. fat
1 c. brown sugar
1 egg
¼ c. sour milk
1¾ c. flour

½ tsp. salt
½ tsp. soda
½ c. nuts, pecans
1 c. candied cherries
1 c. chopped dates

Mix, chill, drop by teaspoon 1 inch apart on greased cookie sheet. Top with ½ pecan or cherry. Bake 350° approximately for 10 minutes.

POTATO CHIP COOKIES

Geraldine Preston

½ lb. butter & ½ lb. margarine
1 c. sugar
2 tsp. vanilla
3 c. flour

¾ c. chopped nuts
1½ c. crushed potato chips,
  stale ones OK

Cream sugar and butter/margarine mixture. Add all other ingredients. Mix together. Drop on cookie sheet teaspoon approximately 1 to 1½ inches plop. Use Silverstone cookie sheet. Bake 350°, 12-15 minutes. Cool, sprinkle powdered sugar. Makes 80 cookies

BEST CHOCOLATE CHIP COOKIE

Luella Pumfery

8 oz. (2 sticks) sweet butter
1 tsp. vanilla
¾ c. light brown sugar, firmly
  packed
2¼ c. flour
1 tsp. hot water
12 oz. (2 c.) chocolate chips

1 tsp. salt
¾ c. granulated sugar
2 c. (large or ex-large)
1 tsp. baking soda
8 oz. (2 generous cups) walnuts,
  cut in pieces

Preheat oven to 375°. Cut foil to fit cookie sheets. Cream the butter, add the salt, vanilla and both sugars and beat well. Add the eggs. Add ½ the flour and scraping bowl with rubber spatula, beat only until incorporated. In a small cup, stir the baking soda into hot water to dissolve it then mix it into the dough. Add the remaining flour and beat only to mix. Remove from mixer and stir in nuts and chocolate chips. Drop by teaspoon or wet your hands, shake off excess water and roll and shape to flatten into a round shape about ½ inch thick and place on foil. Slide a cookie sheet under foil. Bake for 12 minutes or until cookies are browned all over. They must be crisp, do not underbake. Makes 55 (3-inch) cookies.

MELTING MOMENTS
(A Christmas Cookie)

Jean Hansel

¾ c. butter
¼ c. cornstarch

¼ c. confectioners' sugar
1 c. flour

Mix together butter and sugar. Blend in cornstarch and flour. Drop by half teaspoon onto greased cookie sheet. Bake at 350°, 10 to 15 minutes. Cool and frost with frosting, ¼ cup butter, ¼ cup confectioners' sugar, ½ teaspoon vanilla. It can be tinted with food coloring.

QUICK & EASY
(Kids Love Them)

Connie Castor

Melt 1 large package butterscotch chips in double boiler or watch carefully in Teflon coated saucepan. Add 1 can Chinese noodles (like those used in Chop Suey). Drop by teaspoonfuls on wax paper and let cool.

BIRDS NEST COOKIES

Pearl Sarno

½ c. butter
1 egg yolk
Almond extract

¼ c. brown sugar
1 c. flour
Walnuts

Form balls and dip in beaten egg white. Roll in chopped nuts. Press centers. Bake 8 to 10 minutes at 350°. Press a second time and bake 10 minutes more. When cold fill center with jelly or jam.

HUNGARIAN FRUIT PASTRIES

1 pkg. Pillsbury hot roll mix
½ c. oleo or butter
½ c. dairy sour cream
½ tsp. vanilla

2 egg yolks, slightly beaten
½ c. powdered sugar
¼ c. apricot or raspberry
   preserves

Heat oven to 350°. In large bowl, combine hot roll mix and yeast. Add margarine, sour cream, vanilla and eggs; blend until ball forms. Divide into 4 parts. Shape into balls. On lightly powdered sugared surface, roll out each ball into 8-inch circle. Cut each into 12 triangles. Spread ¼ teaspoon preserves on wide end of each. Roll up, starting with wide end. Place point side down on ungreased cookie sheets. Bank for 18 to 23 minutes or until light golden brown around edges. Sift powdered sugar onto paper towels. Place warm pastries on towels. Sprinkle with additional powdered sugar. Makes 48.

66230-05

SNICKERDOODLES

Tony Kisel

Mix together thoroughly:

1 c. shortening

2 eggs

1½ c. sugar

Sift together:

2¾ c. flour

1 tsp. soda

2 tsp. cream of tartar

½ tsp. salt

Chill dough overnight. Roll into balls and then roll in:

2 T. sugar

2 T. cinnamon

Place 2 inches apart on ungreased pan. Bake until light brown, but still soft. Bake 8 to 10 minutes at 400°. Makes 5 to 6 dozen.

COCONUT BARS

Ruth Eisenlohr

⅓ c. oleo

1½ c. brown sugar

1¼ c. flour

1 tsp. vanilla

1 c. chopped nuts

1 can flaked coconut

2 eggs

½ tsp. salt

Cream oleo and ½ cup brown sugar. Add 1 cup flour; mix well. Pat in 9 x 13-inch pan. Bake 375°, 12 minutes. Mix remaining 1 cup brown sugar, ¼ cup flour, blend in eggs, vanilla, nuts and coconut. Spread over baked mixture. Bake at 375° for 15 minutes. Cool and cut into bars.

APRICOT TWISTS

Jean Hansel

2 c. flour

¾ tsp. ground mace

½ tsp. vanilla

½ c. apricot pastry filling

½ c. sugar

1 c. butter or oleo

⅓ to ½ c. ice water

Stir together flour, mace and ½ teaspoon salt. Cut in butter to coarse crumbs. Combine vanilla with 1 tablespoon of the ice water. Toss into flour mixture, add remaining water, a tablespoon at a time, tossing till dough is moistened. Shape into ball; cover. Chill 30 minutes. Divide dough in half. On a lightly floured surface roll each half to 18 x 8 inches. Spread half the apricot filling over half of each rectangle along 8-inch side. Fold plain portion of dough over filling. Trim edges. Cut each rectangle into 18 (4 x 1-inch) strips. Twist strips 3 times. Place on ungreased cookie sheet. Bake at 400° for 15 minutes. Cool. Makes 3 dozen.

PEANUT BUTTER CRISPS

Sara Webber

Cream:

1 c. oleo
1 c. brown sugar

1 c. white sugar

Add:

2 eggs, one at a time
1 tsp. vanilla

1 c. peanut butter

Add:

2½ c. flour
1 tsp. soda

1 tsp. baking powder
1 tsp. salt

Drop by teaspoon on ungreased cookie tin. Bake about 15 minutes at 350° or until golden brown. If desired press peanut halves in top before baking.

GUMDROP COOKIES

Pearl Sarno

1 c. shortening
1 c. granulated sugar
1 tsp. vanilla
1 tsp. baking powder
½ tsp. salt
1 c. coconut

1 c. brown sugar
2 eggs
2 c. flour
½ tsp. soda
2 c. quick Quaker oats
1 c. gumdrops, cut in pieces

Cream shortening and sugars. Add egg and beat well. Sift dry ingredients, add to creamed mixture. Blend. Add oats, coconut and gumdrops. Roll dough into small balls. Place on greased cookie sheets. Press with fork. Bake 10 minutes at 350°. Makes 3 to 6 dozen. Flavor is improved when stored a few days.

COOKIES

Maude Moore

½ c. oleo
1 egg
1¾ c. flour
½ tsp. salt
1 c. candied cherries

1 c. brown sugar
¼ c. sour milk
½ tsp. soda
½ c. nuts
1 c. chopped dates

Mix, chill, drop by teaspoon on greased cookie sheet. Bake 8 to 10 minutes.

66230-05

CHOCOLATE CHIP PUDDING COOKIES

Dean Jones

2¼ c. flour
1 tsp. baking soda
1 c. butter or oleo, softened
¾ c. packed brown sugar
¼ c. sugar
1 (4-serving) pkg. instant
  pudding*

1 tsp. vanilla
2 eggs
1 c. chopped nuts
1 (12-oz.) pkg. chocolate chips

Mix flour with baking soda. Combine butter, the sugars, pudding mix and vanilla in large mixer bowl; beat until smooth and creamy. Beat in eggs. Gradually add flour mixture, then stir in nuts and chocolate chips. Batter will be stiff. Drop from teaspoon onto ungreased cookie sheet; about 2 inches apart. Bake at 375° for 8 to 10 minutes. Makes about 7 dozen. *Pudding suggestions: Butter pecan, butterscotch, chocolate, milk chocolate, chocolate fudge, French vanilla or vanilla flavor. I use French vanilla.

DATE FILLED SQUARES

Ruth Eisenlohr

1⅓ c. rolled oats
1¾ c. flour
½ tsp. soda
½ tsp. salt

1 c. walnuts
1 c. brown sugar
1 tsp. cinnamon
1 c. oleo, melted

Mix all ingredients well stirring in butter last. Pat half on bottom of 9 x 13-inch pan. Spread with date filling. Pat remainder of dough over this. Bake in oven 325° for 30 minutes. Cut while warm. **Date Filling:** Boil 1 pound pitted dates, cut fine with 1 cup sugar, ½ cup water until smooth. Add lemon or orange rind if desired. Cool.

GERMAN ANISE COOKIES

Virginia Kenney

2 eggs
½ tsp. soda, dissolved in 1 T.
  hot water
1 T. whole anise seed

¼ tsp. salt
2 c. flour
½ c. granulated sugar

In large bowl, beat eggs at medium speed of mixer until very light. Gradually add brown sugar, continue beating 15 minutes. Mixture should be very thick. Stir in salt and dissolved soda. Fold in flour and anise seed until well blended. Put sugar in pie plate. With lightly greased or oiled hands (dough will be sticky, do not stir in more flour). Form dough in balls the size of hickory nuts. Roll in sugar to coat. Arrange 1½ inches apart on cookie sheet. Bake in preheated 375° oven, 8 to 10

(continued)

minutes or until light brown. Cookie will puff up during baking, then flatten and crackle on top when done. Cookies are soft when taken from oven, but quickly become firm. About 90.

SOUR CREAM COOKIES

Carolyn Martin

1 c. margarine	3 c. flour
2 eggs	½ tsp. baking powder
1 tsp. vanilla	1½ c. sugar
1 c. sour cream	1 tsp. salt
½ tsp. soda	

Cream margarine and sugar; then add eggs. Sift dry ingredients together and add alternately with sour cream. Bake at 350° for 10 to 15 minutes.

PUMPKIN NUT COOKIES

Dean Jones
From my sister Betty

½ c. shortening	1 tsp. salt
1 c. sugar	2½ tsp. cinnamon
2 eggs	½ tsp. nutmeg
1 c. pumpkin	¼ tsp. ginger
2 c. flour	1 c. raisins
4 tsp. baking powder	1 c. chopped nuts

Cream shortening, add sugar gradually. Cream until light and fluffy. Add eggs and pumpkin; mix well. Sift flour, baking powder, salt and spices together. Stir in dry ingredients and mix until blended. Add raisins and nuts. Drop by teaspoonfuls on greased cookie sheet. Bake in 350° oven for approximately 15 minutes. Makes 4 dozen cookies. May be frozen, if desired.

ORANGE SUGAR COOKIES

Dean Jones
My Mom's

1 c. butter	1 (6-oz.) can frozen pineapple-
1 c. sugar	orange concentrate, thawed
2 eggs	Nuts, opt.
3 c. sifted flour	Cinnamon sugar
1 tsp. soda	

Cream together butter and sugar, add eggs and beat until fluffy. sift together flour and soda and add alternately to creamed mixture with ½ cup juice concentrate. Drop from teaspoon, 2 inches apart onto un-greased cookie sheet. Bake in preheated 400° oven from about 8

(continued)

66230-05

minutes or until lightly browned around edges. Brush hot cookies with remaining juice. Sprinkle with cinnamon sugar. Cool cookies.

GOLDEN CARROT COOKIES

Helen Seys

1 c. shortening	2 c. flour
³/₄ c. sugar	2 tsp. baking powder
2 eggs	¹/₂ tsp. salt
1 c. mashed cooked carrots	³/₄ c. coconut

Heat oven to 400°. Mix shortening, sugar, eggs and carrots. Measure flour, baking powder and salt and blend into shortening mixture. Mix in coconut. Drop dough by teaspoonfuls about 2 inches apart on lightly greased baking sheet. Bake 8 to 10 minutes. Makes 4 dozen cookies. Frost with Orange Butter Icing:

2¹/₂ T. soft butter	1¹/₂ T. orange juice
1¹/₂ c. confectioners' sugar	2 tsp. grated orange rind

Blend butter and sugar together. Stir in orange juice and grated orange rind until smooth.

DATE PINWHEELS

Doris Crawford

2 c. brown sugar	3 eggs, beaten
4 c. flour	1 tsp. salt
1 c. shortening	¹/₂ tsp. soda

Filling:

1 lb. dates, cut up	1 c. white sugar
1 c. water	

Cook till thick. Roll dough out and spread date mixture and nuts on top. Roll it up like a jelly roll and put in refrigerator for 2 or 3 days. Cut slices and bake at 375°.

LEBKUCHEN
(Germany)

Jean Hansel

2¾ c. all-purpose flour, sifted
½ tsp. soda
1 tsp. cinnamon
½ tsp. cloves
½ tsp. nutmeg
1 c. honey
1 tsp. grated lemon rind
1 T. lemon juice
1 c. powdered sugar

2 T. water
1 (8-oz.) ctn. mixed candied
   fruits, finely chopped
1 c. chopped walnuts
1 egg
Candied red & green cherries,
   halved
Blanched almonds, halved

Sift flour, soda, cinnamon, cloves and nutmeg in large bowl. Stir in fruits and nuts. Beat egg slightly in a small bowl. Stir in honey, grated lemon rind and juice. Stir into flour mixture to make a soft dough. Divide dough in half. Moisten palm of hand with water. Press and flatten each half of dough on a greased and floured cookie sheet to a 12 x 8-inch rectangle, ⅛-inch thick. Bake at 400° for 12 minutes or until firm and lightly browned. Remove from oven to wire rack. Combine powdered sugar and water in a small bowl. Spread over warm cookies. Cut into squares. Decorate with candied cherries and almonds before frosting sets. Cool before storing in tightly covered container.

FINSKA PINNAR
(Finland)

Jean Hansel

1 c. (2 sticks) unsalted butter,
   softened
½ c. sugar
1 tsp. almond extract
1⅔ c. all-purpose flour, sifted
½ c. finely chopped blanched
   almonds

3 T. sugar
1 egg yolk
1 T. water
2 squares semi-sweet chocolate
2 tsp. vegetable shortening
Royal frosting or powdered
   sugar & water

Beat butter with ½ cup sugar and almond extract in a large bowl with electric mixer until light and fluffy. Stir in flour until soft dough forms. Refrigerate at least one hour. Combine almonds and the 3 tablespoons sugar on wax paper. Beat egg yolk and water until blended. Pinch off about 2 teaspoons of dough for each cookie. Roll with floured hands to a 3-inch length, about the thickness of a little finger. Brush cookies with egg mixture; dip tops in nut mixture. Place 2 inches apart on ungreased cookie sheets. Bake at 375° for 12 minutes or until golden brown (cookies will flatten into ovals during baking). Cool on wire racks. **To decorate:** Melt chocolate with shortening; cool slightly. Drizzle over cookies. Thin a small amount of Royal Frosting with milk and drizzle over chocolate. Let set.

(continued)

66230-05

Royal Frosting:

1 egg white	1¾ c. powdered sugar
⅛ tsp. cream of tartar	

Beat egg white with cream of tartar. Add powdered sugar.

SNICKERDOODLES

LIll Gurr

Mix:

1 c. oleo	1½ c. sugar
2 eggs	

Sift together:

2¾ c. flour	½ tsp. salt
2 tsp. cream of tartar	1 tsp. soda

Chill; roll into balls size of a walnut; roll mix in 2 tablespoons sugar and cinnamon. Place 2 inches apart. Bake 400°, 8 to 10 minutes.

PUMPKIN COOKIES

Louella Pumfery

½ c. butter or oleo	½ c. diced almonds, toasted
1 egg	1½ c. sugar
1 tsp. vanilla	1 c. cooked pumpkin
1 tsp. baking powder	2½ c. flour
½ tsp. salt	1 tsp. soda
1 tsp. cinnamon or 2 tsp. pumpkin pie spice	1 tsp. nutmeg
	1 c. chocolate chips

Cream together butter and sugar until light and fluffy. Beat in egg, pumpkin and vanilla. Mix flour, baking powder, soda, salt and spices. Add to mixture and mix well. Add nuts and chocolate chips with heavy spoon; mix well. Drop by teaspoonfuls onto greased cookie sheet. Bake at 350° for 15 minutes or until light brown. Makes 6 dozen.

MOCA-NUT BUTTERBALLS

Sara Webber

1 c. softened butter or oleo	1 T. instant coffee
2 tsp. vanilla	1⅔ c. flour
⅓ c. unsweetened cocoa	2 c. finely chopped walnuts or pecans
½ tsp. salt	Confectioners' sugar
½ c. sugar	

In large bowl of electric mixer, cream butter with sugar and vanilla until light and fluffy. Add instant coffee, cocoa, flour and salt. Blend well. Stir

(continued)

in nuts. Shape into 1-inch balls and place 1½ inches apart on lightly greased baking sheet. Bake at 325° for 15 minutes. Remove to wire rack to cool. When cookies are cooled, sprinkle with confectioners' sugar. Store in airtight container. Makes 3 dozen.

SOUR CREAM COOKIES

Carolyn Martin

1 c. margarine	½ tsp. baking powder
2 eggs	1½ c. sugar
1 tsp. vanilla	1 tsp. salt
1 c. sour cream	¼ tsp. soda
3 c. flour	

Cream margarine and sugar; then add eggs. Sift dry ingredients together and add alternately with sour cream. Bake at 350° for 10 to 15 minutes.

FREEZER COOKIES

Zetta Taylor

3 c. all-purpose flour	1½ tsp. soda
2 tsp. salt	

Add:

2 c. soft shortening	2 eggs
1 c. granulated sugar	2 tsp. vanilla
1 c. firmly packed brown sugar	

Mix until smooth, about 2 minutes. Stir in 3 cups rolled oats (quick or regular). Add 1 cup cut up nuts, if desired. Divide dough into 4 parts. Shape each into 8- to 10-inch long roll. Wrap in waxed paper or foil. Chill several hours or overnight. Cut into ⅛-inch slices. Place on ungreased cookie sheet about 2 inches apart. Bake about 10 minutes in moderate oven (350°). Makes about 10 dozen cookies. May be frozen in heavy weight foil as soon as mixed. Label. Dough can be cut when frozen, but likely to crumble. For neat cookies, let dough partially thaw before slicing.

REF. TEA COOKIES

Lill Gurr

1 c. shortening or margarine	3½ c. all-purpose flour
2 c. light brown sugar	1 tsp. baking soda
2 eggs	½ tsp. salt
1 tsp. vanilla	
1 c. chopped black walnuts, any nuts are OK	

(continued)

66230-05

Cream shortening and sugar thoroughly. Add unbeaten eggs and mix well. Add vanilla and nuts. Sift flour, baking soda and salt together three times. Add to mixture and mix all well. Form into rolls 1½ thick and refrigerate for several hours. Slice 1½-inch thick. Bake on ungreased cookie sheet 10 to 12 minutes at 400°. Makes 10 dozen cookies.

PUMPKIN BARS

Lill Gurr

2 c. flour	2 c. sugar
2 tsp. baking soda	1 c. nuts, opt.
¼ tsp. salt	1 c. salad oil
2 tsp. cinnamon	4 eggs, beaten
1 tsp. pumpkin spice	2 c. pumpkin

Combine all ingredients in large bowl. Blend and pour into lightly greased 17 x 11-inch baking sheet. Bake at 350° for 25 to 30 minutes.

Frost:

4 oz. cream cheese	2 c. powdered sugar
3 T. margarine	1 tsp. milk
½ tsp. vanilla	

Beat until smooth.

JAM TARTS

Sara Webber

Cream:

1 c. butter or margarine	2 eggs
1 c. peanut butter	2 tsp. vanilla
2 c. sugar	

Sift Together:

2½ c. flour	½ tsp. salt
1 tsp. baking powder	

Stir dry ingredients into creamed mixture. Chill several hours. Roll dough on floured board to ⅛ inch thickness. Cut with cookie cutter. Put 1 teaspoon jam in center of ½ of the cookies. Cut center out of other ½ of cookies with center of doughnut cutter. Place on top of cookies with jam and secure outside edges. Bake on greased cookie sheet for 10 to 12 minutes at 350°. Cook for a few minutes on cookie sheet before removing. Makes 4 dozen cookies.

TROPICAL CHRISTMAS COOKIE

Muriel Glendenning

1 c. shortening
1¼ c. sugar
1 tsp. salt
1 tsp. grated lemon rind
2 tsp. grated orange rind

1 T. lemon juice
2 eggs, unbeaten
2¼ c. flour
2⅓ c. coconut
1 c. mixed candied fruits

Combine shortening, sugar, salt, rinds, juice and eggs and beat thoroughly. Add flour to first mixture and mix well. Add coconut and mixed fruits and blend. Drop rounded tablespoons of dough on greased baking sheet. Bake at 375° for 12-15 minutes. Makes 3 dozen.

MAGIC COOKIE BARS

Ruth Eisenlohr

½ c. butter
1 (14-oz.) can Eagle Brand milk,
  sweetened condensed
1 (6-oz.) pkg. chocolate morsels

1 (3½-oz.) can flaked coconut
1 c. nuts, chopped
1½ c. graham cracker crumbs

Melt butter or oleo in pan and sprinkle crumbs over it. Pour sweetened condensed milk over crumbs. Top evenly with chocolate chips and coconut and nuts. Bake in 13 x 9-inch pan in 350° oven for 30 minutes. Loosely cover any leftovers.

RAISIN FILLED COOKIE

Virginia Kenney

4 c. flour
1 tsp. baking powder
1 tsp. baking soda
½ tsp. salt
¼ tsp. nutmeg

1 c. sugar
1 c. packed light brown sugar
3 eggs
2 tsp. vanilla
1 c. butter or oleo

Mix dry ingredients, cut in butter, add beaten eggs with vanilla. Add to the flour mixture and mix with fork until a smooth dough. Chill several hours or overnight. Divide dough in several portions. On floured board roll dough to ⅛ inch thickness. Cut with floured 2-inch cutter. Put scant teaspoon of filling in center then top with another circle. Press edges together with a fork. Bake 1½ inches apart on ungreased cookie sheet at 375° for 10 to 12 minutes or until golden brown. Makes 66 cookies.
Filling: Mix well ¾ cup sugar, 1 tablespoon cornstarch. In small pan, heat 1 cup water and 2 cups seedless raisins to boiling. Add sugar mixture and boil gently until mixture is clear and thick and raisins are plump. When cool add 1 teaspoon vanilla.

66230-05

CHOCOLATE DROP COOKIES

Inez Brimhall

2 c. pastry flour
1½ tsp. baking powder
½ tsp. salt
½ tsp. soda
½ c. butter
⅔ c. brown sugar, packed

1 egg
2 (1-oz.) squares unsweetened
  chocolate, melted
½ c. milk
½ c. broken nut meats
1 tsp. vanilla

Sift the flour, measure then sift again 3 times with the baking powder, salt and soda. Cream the butter and sugar together until very light and fluffy. Beat in the egg and chocolate mixing well. Now add flour alternately with the milk stirring to smoothness after each addition. Blend in the nuts and vanilla and drop the batter from a teaspoon onto an ungreased baking sheet. Bake in moderate oven, 350° for 12-14 minutes or until done. Frost with a chocolate icing or any fruity butter frosting.

NOEL BALLS

Lill Gurr

1 c. butter
5 T. confectioners' sugar
2 c. flour

2 tsp. vanilla
1½ c. chopped nuts

Cream butter and confectioners' sugar; work flour, vanilla and nuts into creamed mixture. Form into desired shapes. Cook on ungreased baking sheet at 350° for 30 minutes. Roll in powdered sugar when slightly cooled. Serves 5 to 6 dozen.

CHOCOLATE CHIP PUDDING COOKIES

Madeline Cramer

2¼ c. flour
1 tsp. baking soda
1 c. butter or oleo, softened
¾ c. packed brown sugar
¼ c. sugar
1 (4-serving) pkg. instant
  pudding*

1 tsp. vanilla
2 eggs
1 (12-oz.) pkg. chocolate chips
1 c. chopped nuts, opt.

Mix flour with baking soda; set aside. Combine butter, the sugars, pudding and vanilla in large mixer bowl; beat until smooth and creamy. Beat in eggs. Gradually add flour mixture, then stir in nuts and chips. Batter will be stiff. Drop from teaspoon onto ungreased baking sheet about 2 inches apart. Bake at 375° for 8 to 10 minutes.

DATE BALLS

Ruth Eisenlohr

½ c. butter or oleo
1 c. sugar

2 eggs, beaten
1 (11-oz.) pkg. dates, cut up

Melt butter or oleo in frying pan; add sugar and eggs and dates. Cook 8 to 10 minutes until dates are cooked and mixture thickens. Remove and add 2 cups Rice Krispies to half box. Butter hands and make small balls. Roll in coconut.

ZUCCHINI COOKIES

Dean Jones

½ c. oleo
1 c. sugar

1 egg
1 peeled or unpeeled zucchini

Cream together and then add 1 cup grated zucchini. Add 2 cups flour, 1 teaspoon soda, 1 teaspoon cinnamon, ½ teaspoon cloves and ½ teaspoon salt. Add 1 cup chopped walnuts. Drop by spoonfuls into Pam sprayed cookie sheet. Bake at 375° for 12-15 minutes.

Cream Cheese Frosting:

3 oz. cream cheese
¼ c. oleo

2 c. powdered sugar

Cream together and spread on cooled cookies.

Recipe Favorites

66230-05

THIS
&
THAT

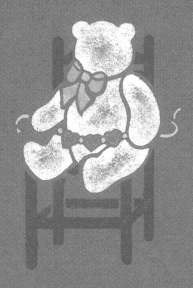

*But the fruit of the Spirit is love, joy,
peace, patience, kindness, goodness,
faithfulness, gentleness and self-control.
Against such things there is no law.*

~ Galatians 5:22, 23

Helpful Hints

- To refinish antiques or revitalize wood, use equal parts of linseed oil, white vinegar, and turpentine. Rub into the furniture or wood with a soft cloth and lots of elbow grease.

- To stop the ants in your pantry, seal off cracks where they are entering with putty or petroleum jelly. Also, try sprinkling red pepper on floors and counter tops.

- To fix sticking sliding doors, windows, and drawers, rub wax along their tracks.

- To make a simple polish for copper bottom cookware, mix equal parts of flour and salt with vinegar to create a paste. Store the paste in the refrigerator.

- Applying baking soda on a damp sponge will remove starch deposits from an iron. Make sure the iron is cold and unplugged.

- Remove stale odors in the wash by adding baking soda.

- To clean Teflon™, combine 1 cup water, 2 tablespoons baking soda and ½ cup liquid bleach. Boil in stained pan for 5 to 10 minutes or until the stain disappears. Wash, rinse, dry, and condition with oil before using the pan again.

- Corning Ware can be cleaned by filling it with water and dropping in two denture cleaning tablets. Let stand for 30 to 45 minutes.

- A little instant coffee will work wonders on your wood furniture. Just make a thick paste from instant coffee and a little water, and rub it into the nicks and scratches on your dark wood furniture. You'll be amazed at how new and beautiful those pieces will look.

- For a clogged shower head, boil it for 15 minutes in a mixture of ½ cup vinegar and 1 quart water.

- For a spicy aroma, toss dried orange or lemon rinds into the fireplace.

- Add raw rice to the salt shaker to keep the salt free-flowing.

- Ice cubes will help sharpen garbage disposal blades.

- Separate stuck-together glasses by filling the inside one with cold water and setting them in hot water.

THIS & THAT

RHUBARB JAM

Nancy Cramer

5 c. cut-up rhubarb
4 c. sugar

1½ pkg. strawberry or raspberry
Jello = ⅔ c.

Cook rhubarb and sugar and bring to a boil and gently boil for 10 minutes. Take off burner, add Jello and stir until well mixed. Skim off foam and pour into jars and seal. Makes about 8 jelly jars.

RASPBERRY JAM

Pauline Hoadley

5 c. green tomatoes, ground & save juice

3½ c. sugar

Bring to a boil and boil for 15 minutes. Add 2 small boxes raspberry Jello. Stir well. Put into jars and seal.

SIMPLE GUACAMOLE

Londa Wines

2 med. ripe avocados
1 T. lemon juice

¼ c. chunky salsa
⅛ to ½ tsp. salt

Peel and chop avocados; place in a small bowl, sprinkle with lemon juice. Add salsa and salt; mash coarsely with fork. Yields: 1½ cups. Refrigerate.

SPINACH DIP

Jerry Swagler

1 pkg. chopped frozen spinach
1 can slivered water chestnuts
3 green onions, chopped

1 pkg. Knorr vegetable soup mix
1 c. sour cream
1 c. mayonnaise

Mix above and put in a hollowed round pumpernickel loaf.

CREAMY HORSERADISH DIP

Donna Swagler

1 (8 oz.) cream cheese
½ c. mayonnaise
⅓ c. horseradish sauce

¼ c. green onion, chopped
4 T. bacon, chopped

(continued)

Combine cheese, mayonnaise and horseradish until well blended. Stir in green onion and bacon. Serve with vegetables or chips.

CHEESE WAFERS

Donna Swagler

2 sticks oleo	½ tsp. pepper
2 c. flour	½ tsp. salt
8 oz. sharp cheese, grated	2 c. Rice Krispies

Cut oleo in flour; mix in cheese, pepper and salt. Fold in Rice Krispies and mix thoroughly. Roll into rolls and refrigerate. Slice medium thickness and bake at 350° for 15 minutes. Stick can be frozen and baked as needed.

CHEESE BALL DELIGHT

Carolyn Stuckum

2 (8-oz.) pkgs. cream cheese	2 T. minced onion, dry
¼ c. green pepper, finely chopped	1 T. Lawry's seasoning salt
1 (8 oz.) crushed pineapple, well drained	Dash of black pepper
	Chopped nuts

Mix together all ingredients, except nuts. Shape into ball. Refrigerate until firm. Roll in chopped nuts.

PIGS-IN-A BLANKET

2 (8-oz.) cans refrigerated quick crescent dinner rolls	1 (16-oz.) pkg. cocktail franks
2 T. grainy, Dijon or honey mustard	Ketchup, mustard or prepared horseradish

Preheat oven to 375°. Working with one package of rolls at a time, separate dough into 8 triangles. Cut each triangle into thirds lengthwise. Spread each triangle with mustard. Place one cocktail frank on widest end of triangle and roll up tightly. Place on ungreased cookie sheet, point side down. Repeat with remaining dough and cocktail franks. Bake pigs-in-a-blanket in preheated oven for 12-15 minutes or until golden brown. Serve warm with extra mustard, ketchup or prepared horseradish. **Make-ahead tip:** Prepare and bake pigs-in-a-blanket up to a week ahead. Freeze in plastic food-storage bags. To reheat: place pigs, thawed on cookie sheet, cover loosely with foil and bake at 350° for about 10 minutes. Makes 48 pigs.

66230-05

PARTY CHEESE BALL

Edwina Watkins

2 lg. pkgs. soft cream cheese
3 green onions, chopped
2 T. lemon juice

4-5 dashes garlic salt
1 pkg. chopped beef, chopped
  into small pieces

Mix the above ingredients together and form into ball. Roll in nuts if desired. Chill and enjoy.

OVEN CARAMEL POPCORN

Connie Castor

2 c. brown sugar
½ c. corn syrup
1 tsp. salt
1 tsp. butter flavoring
2 sticks oleo

6 qt. popped corn
1 tsp. soda
Nutmeats, pecans, walnuts,
  peanuts, cashews, etc.

Boil brown sugar, butter, syrup and salt for 5 minutes. Remove from heat and add baking soda and butter flavoring. Stir well over popped corn and nuts and spread on cookie sheets. Place in 200° oven for 1 hour, stirring every 15 minutes. Remove from oven and let cool. Store in covered container to keep crisp.

VEGGIE BARS

Pauline Hoadley

2 pkgs. crescent refrigerator
  rolls

Spread rolls out on cookie sheet (do not separate); bake and cool.

¾ c. Miracle Whip
8 oz. cream cheese

1 pkg. Hidden Valley Ranch
  dressing

Whip all ingredients together. Spread over baked and cooled crescent rolls. Top with any kind of raw vegetables. Sprinkle one (8-ounce) package shredded cheddar cheese over vegetables. Cut and serve.

CRACKER JACK

Inez Brimhall

1 c. brown sugar
1 T. butter, add last

1 c. white Karo

Let sugar and Karo cook until it forms a soft ball, add butter and stir into:

1 c. ground peanuts
1 c. ground popcorn

1 tsp. lemon flavoring

(continued)

Dip hands in cold water and press mixture into buttered pan.

CRANBERRY RELISH

Hazel Cramer

1 pkg. lemon Jello
1 orange
1 c. cranberries
½ c. celery, chop fine

1 c. boiling water
1 c. sugar
1 c. nuts, if desired

Grind together.

MELTING MOMENTS

Gary Hansel

¾ c. butter
¼ c. cornstarch

¼ c. confectioners' sugar
1 c. flour

Mix together butter and sugar. Blend in cornstarch and flour. Drop by half teaspoon onto greased cookie sheet. Bake at 350°, 10-15 minutes. Cool and frost.

Frosting:

¼ c. butter
¼ c. confectioners' sugar

½ tsp. vanilla

BACON WRAPS

Dean Jones

1 can water chestnuts
1 lb. bacon, cut in thirds, not
 thick sliced

Cut water chestnuts in half. Wrap with bacon, secure with toothpick. Bake at 400° for 25 to 30 minutes. Drain grease.

Sauce:

½ c. brown sugar

½ c. catsup

Mix above ingredients and drizzle over bacon wraps and heat in 325° oven for 15 to 20 minutes. Good.

ELEPHANT EARS

Dean Jones

1½ c. milk
2 T. sugar
1 tsp. salt
6 T. shortening

2 pkgs. dry yeast
4 c. flour
Oil for frying ears

(continued)

66230-05

In saucepan combine milk, sugar, salt and shortening; heat until shortening is melted. Do not boil. Cool mixture to lukewarm. Add yeast and stir until dissolved; stir in flour, two cups at a time. Beat after each addition until smooth. Put in a greased bowl, cover with damp cloth and let rise until doubled about 30 minutes. Dust hands with flour. Pinch off pieces of dough about the size of golf balls. Stretch each into a thin 6- to 8-inch circle. Fry one at a time in 350° oil until dough rises to the surface. Turn and fry other side until light brown. Drain on paper towel and sprinkle generously with sugar mixture. **Sugar mixture:** Combine ½ cup sugar with 1 teaspoon cinnamon. These are so good with applesauce with red cinnamon candies melted into it. Just spread it on.

MINI PASTRIES

Ginger Swagler

Dough:

2 (8-oz.) pkgs. cream cheese, softened	**1 lb. butter, soft**
	4 c. flour

Filling:

1 lb. ground beef round steak	**1 (10¾-oz.) can condensed**
1 env. dry onion soup mix	**cream mushroom soup**

In medium bowl, combine cream cheese, butter and flour until thoroughly blended. Wrap in plastic wrap, refrigerate until chilled. Heat oven to 400°. In small skillet, brown beef; drain well. Stir in onion soup mix and mushroom soup; set aside. On lightly floured cloth, roll out dough circles (cookie cutter). Three inch place ½ teaspoon filling on half of each circle, fold other half over. Press edge with fork to seal. Place on ungreased cookie sheet. Bake about 15 minutes. Makes 75-100 appetizers. Pastries can be frozen before or after baking.

PLAY DOUGH

Hazel Cramer

1 c. salt	**2 T. salad oil**
2 c. flour	**Food coloring**
1 c. water	

Add more flour if needed until dough isn't sticky.

BUDGET FRUIT PUNCH

Sandy Whaley

1 pkg. cherry Kool-Aid, sugar-
  free
2 qt. water
1 (No. 3) can Hawaiian punch,
  red

1 (No. 3) can pineapple juice
1 qt. ginger ale, chilled, add last

Mix Kool-Aid, sugar and water then add rest of ingredients.

Recipe Favorites

84

INDEX OF RECIPES

SOUR CREAM BLUEBERRY
BREAD   30

DESSERTS

AMAZING COCONUT PIE   52
APPLE WALNUT CAKE   38
APPLESAUCE CAKE   39
AUNT GLORIA'S CARROT
CAKE   43
BANKET   33
BIBLE CAKE   49
BLUEBERRY BUCKLE   50
BLUEBERRY COFFEE CAKE   42
BLUEBERRY CREAM CHEESE
PIE   53
BLUEBERRY MUFFINS   48
BLUEBERRY SOUR CREAM
CAKE   34
BLUEBERRY STREUSEL
COFFEE CAKE   51
BROWNIE TYPE CAKE   37
BUTTERSCOTCH SQUARES   35
CHERRIES IN THE SNOW   49
CHERRY CRUNCH OR OTHER
FRUIT   50
COCONUT PINEAPPLE   42
COFFEE CAKE   34
CRAZY CAKE   41
DUMP CAKE   38
EASY CHOCOLATE DESSERT   35
EASY SOUTHERN BANANA
PUDDING   45
FRENCH CHERRY DESSERT   36
FRESH APPLE CAKE   44
FRESH STRAWBERRY PIE   52
FRUIT COCKTAIL CAKE   46
FRUIT CRUMB PIE BARS   53
FRUIT MAGIC   48
HEAVENLY DELIGHT   50
IMPOSSIBLE PIE   37
INSTANT RICE PUDDING   47
KIM'S EASY DESSERT   47
LEMON BARS   45
LEMON-CRANBERRY BARS   46
MAGGIE'S CHOCOLATE
BROWNIES   36
MIRACLE WHIP PINEAPPLE
CAKE   43
MOON CAKE   44
NANCY'S APPLE CAKE   40
NO COOK FROSTING   51
ORANGE PINEAPPLE DELIGHT
CAKE   41
PEACH COBBLER   44
PEANUT BUTTER CHOCOLATE
BARS   47

PEANUT BUTTER FUDGE
CAKE   40
PERFECT PIE CRUST   39
PETER PETER PUMPKIN BARS   41
PINA COLADA CAKE   49
PINEAPPLE CAKE   38
PINEAPPLE CAKE   37
PINEAPPLE CAKE   33
QUICK JELLO DESSERT   49
SEVEN-LAYER BARS   34
7-UP CAKE   34
SOUR CREAM PUMPKIN
COFFEE CAKE HOMEMADE
WITH LOVE   48
SPEEDY APPLE CRISP   42
STRAWBERRY RHUBARB
CRUNCH   52
TEXAS FLAT CAKE   36
TONI KISEL'S APPLE CAKE   46
UGLY DUCKLING CAKE   52
WALDORF SALAD CAKE   33
WHIP CREAM FROSTING   51
YOGURT LEMON PIE   45
ZUCCHINI RING   35
ZUCCHINI SQUASH CAKE   39

COOKIES & CANDY

APRICOT TWISTS   67
BEST CHOCOLATE CHIP
COOKIE   65
BIRDS NEST COOKIES   66
BLACK WALNUT WAFERS   59
BOHEMIAN COOKIES   62
BON-BON CANDY   57
BROWNIES   60
CHEESE DANISH   61
CHOCOLATE CHIP COOKIES   55
CHOCOLATE CHIP PUDDING
COOKIES   77
CHOCOLATE CHIP PUDDING
COOKIES   69
CHOCOLATE DROP COOKIES   77
CHOCOLATE GLAZED
OATMEAL BARS   59
CHRISTMAS CANDY   57
COCONUT BARS   67
COOKIES   68
COOKIES   56
COWBOY COOKIES   55
CRACKER JACK   58
CREAM CHEESE COOKIES   56
CREAM CHEESE COOKIES   60
DATE BALLS   78
DATE FILLED SQUARES   69
DATE PINWHEELS   71
FINSKA PINNAR   72
FORGOTTEN COOKIES   59

THIS & THAT

Cooking Tips

1. After stewing a chicken, cool in broth before cutting into chunks; it will have twice the flavor.

2. To slice meat into thin strips, as for stir-fry dishes, partially freeze it so it will slice more easily.

3. A roast with the bone in will cook faster than a boneless roast. The bone carries the heat to the inside more quickly.

4. When making a roast, place dry onion soup mix in the bottom of your roaster pan. After removing the roast, add 1 can of mushroom soup and you will have a good brown gravy.

5. For a juicier hamburger, add cold water to the beef before grilling (½ cup to 1 pound of meat).

6. To freeze meatballs, place them on a cookie sheet until frozen. Place in plastic bags. They will stay separated so that you may remove as many as you want.

7. To keep cauliflower white while cooking, add a little milk to the water.

8. When boiling corn, add sugar to the water instead of salt. Salt will toughen the corn.

9. To ripen tomatoes, put them in a brown paper bag in a dark pantry, and they will ripen.

10. To keep celery crisp, stand it upright in a pitcher of cold, salted water and refrigerate.

11. When cooking cabbage, place a small tin cup or can half full of vinegar on the stove near the cabbage. It will absorb the odor.

12. Potatoes soaked in salt water for 20 minutes before baking will bake more rapidly.

13. Let raw potatoes stand in cold water for at least a half-hour before frying in order to improve the crispness of French-fried potatoes. Dry potatoes thoroughly before adding to oil.

14. Use greased muffin tins as molds when baking stuffed green peppers.

15. A few drops of lemon juice in the water will whiten boiled potatoes.

16. Buy mushrooms before they "open." When stems and caps are attached firmly, mushrooms are truly fresh.

17. Do not use metal bowls when mixing salads. Use wood, glass or china.

18. Lettuce keeps better if you store it in the refrigerator without washing it. Keep the leaves dry. Wash lettuce the day you are going to use it.

19. Do not use soda to keep vegetables green. It destroys Vitamin C.

20. Do not despair if you oversalt gravy. Stir in some instant mashed potatoes to repair the damage. Just add a little more liquid in order to offset the thickening.

Herbs & Spices

Acquaint yourself with herbs and spices. Add in small amounts, ¼ teaspoon for every 4 servings. Crush dried herbs or snip fresh ones before using. Use 3 times more fresh herbs if substituting fresh for dried.

Basil
Sweet, warm flavor with an aromatic odor. Use whole or ground. Good with lamb, fish, roast, stews, ground beef, vegetables, dressing and omelets.

Bay Leaves
Pungent flavor. Use whole leaf but remove before serving. Good in vegetable dishes, seafood, stews and pickles.

Caraway
Spicy taste and aromatic smell. Use in cakes, breads, soups, cheese and sauerkraut.

Chives
Sweet, mild flavor like that of onion. Excellent in salads, fish, soups and potatoes.

Cilantro
Use fresh. Excellent in salads, fish, chicken, rice, beans and Mexican dishes.

Curry Powder
Spices are combined to proper proportions to give a distinct flavor to meat, poultry, fish and vegetables.

Dill
Both seeds and leaves are flavorful. Leaves may be used as a garnish or cooked with fish, soup, dressings, potatoes and beans. Leaves or the whole plant may be used to flavor pickles.

Fennel
Sweet, hot flavor. Both seeds and leaves are used. Use in small quantities in pies and baked goods. Leaves can be boiled with fish.

Ginger
A pungent root, this aromatic spice is sold fresh, dried or ground. Use in pickles, preserves, cakes, cookies, soups and meat dishes.

Herbs & Spices

Marjoram   May be used both dried or green. Use to flavor fish, poultry, omelets, lamb, stew, stuffing and tomato juice.

Mint   Aromatic with a cool flavor. Excellent in beverages, fish, lamb, cheese, soup, peas, carrots, and fruit desserts.

Oregano   Strong, aromatic odor. Use whole or ground in tomato juice, fish, eggs, pizza, omelets, chili, stew, gravy, poultry and vegetables.

Paprika   A bright red pepper, this spice is used in meat, vegetables and soups or as a garnish for potatoes, salads or eggs.

Parsley   Best when used fresh, but can be used dried as a garnish or as a seasoning. Try in fish, omelets, soup, meat, stuffing and mixed greens.

Rosemary   Very aromatic. Can be used fresh or dried. Season fish, stuffing, beef, lamb, poultry, onions, eggs, bread and potatoes. Great in dressings.

Saffron   Orange-yellow in color, this spice flavors or colors foods. Use in soup, chicken, rice and breads.

Sage   Use fresh or dried. The flowers are sometimes used in salads. May be used in tomato juice, fish, omelets, beef, poultry, stuffing, cheese spreads and breads.

Tarragon   Leaves have a pungent, hot taste. Use to flavor sauces, salads, fish, poultry, tomatoes, eggs, green beans, carrots and dressings.

Thyme   Sprinkle leaves on fish or poultry before broiling or baking. Throw a few sprigs directly on coals shortly before meat is finished grilling.

Baking Breads

Hints for Baking Breads

1. Kneading dough for 30 seconds after mixing improves the texture of baking powder biscuits.

2. Instead of shortening, use cooking or salad oil in waffles and hot cakes.

3. When bread is baking, a small dish of water in the oven will help keep the crust from hardening.

4. Dip a spoon in hot water to measure shortening, butter, etc., and the fat will slip out more easily.

5. Small amounts of leftover corn may be added to pancake batter for variety.

6. To make bread crumbs, use the fine cutter of a food grinder and tie a large paper bag over the spout in order to prevent flying crumbs.

7. When you are doing any sort of baking, you get better results if you remember to preheat your cookie sheet, muffin tins or cake pans.

Rules for Use of Leavening Agents

1. In simple flour mixtures, use 2 teaspoons baking powder to leaven 1 cup flour. Reduce this amount 1/2 teaspoon for each egg used.

2. To 1 teaspoon soda use 2 1/4 teaspoons cream of tartar, 2 cups freshly soured milk, or 1 cup molasses.

3. To substitute soda and an acid for baking powder, divide the amount of baking powder by 4. Take that as your measure and add acid according to rule 2.

Proportions of Baking Powder to Flour

biscuits	to 1 cup flour use 1 1/4 tsp. baking powder
cake with oil	to 1 cup flour use 1 tsp. baking powder
muffins	to 1 cup flour use 1 1/2 tsp. baking powder
popovers	to 1 cup flour use 1 1/4 tsp. baking powder
waffles	to 1 cup flour use 1 1/4 tsp. baking powder

Proportions of Liquid to Flour

drop batter	to 1 cup liquid use 2 to 2 1/2 cups flour
pour batter	to 1 cup liquid use 1 cup flour
soft dough	to 1 cup liquid use 3 to 3 1/2 cups flour
stiff dough	to 1 cup liquid use 4 cups flour

Time and Temperature Chart

Breads	Minutes	Temperature
biscuits	12 - 15	400° - 450°
cornbread	25 - 30	400° - 425°
gingerbread	40 - 50	350° - 370°
loaf	50 - 60	350° - 400°
nut bread	50 - 75	350°
popovers	30 - 40	425° - 450°
rolls	20 - 30	400° - 450°

Baking Desserts

Perfect Cookies

Cookie dough that is to be rolled is much easier to handle after it has been refrigerated for 10 to 30 minutes. This keeps the dough from sticking, even though it may be soft. If not done, the soft dough may require more flour and too much flour makes cookies hard and brittle. Place on a floured board only as much dough as can be easily managed. Flour the rolling pin slightly and roll lightly to desired thickness. Cut shapes close together and add trimmings to dough that needs to be rolled. Place pans or sheets in upper third of oven. Watch cookies carefully while baking in order to avoid burned edges. When sprinkling sugar on cookies, try putting it into a salt shaker in order to save time.

Perfect Pies

1. Pie crust will be better and easier to make if all the ingredients are cool.

2. The lower crust should be placed in the pan so that it covers the surface smoothly. Air pockets beneath the surface will push the crust out of shape while baking.

3. Folding the top crust over the lower crust before crimping will keep juices in the pie.

4. In making custard pie, bake at a high temperature for about ten minutes to prevent a soggy crust. Then finish baking at a low temperature.

5. When making cream pie, sprinkle crust with powdered sugar in order to prevent it from becoming soggy.

Perfect Cakes

1. Fill cake pans two-thirds full and spread batter into corners and sides, leaving a slight hollow in the center.

2. Cake is done when it shrinks from the sides of the pan or if it springs back when touched lightly with the finger.

3. After removing a cake from the oven, place it on a rack for about five minutes. Then, the sides should be loosened and the cake turned out on a rack in order to finish cooling.

4. Do not frost cakes until thoroughly cool.

5. Icing will remain where you put it if you sprinkle cake with powdered sugar first.

Time and Temperature Chart

Dessert	Time	Temperature
butter cake, layer	20-40 min.	380° - 400°
butter cake, loaf	40-60 min.	360° - 400°
cake, angel	50-60 min.	300° - 360°
cake, fruit	3-4 hrs.	275° - 325°
cake, sponge	40-60 min.	300° - 350°
cookies, molasses	18-20 min.	350° - 375°
cookies, thin	10-12 min.	380° - 390°
cream puffs	45-60 min.	300° - 350°
meringue	40-60 min.	250° - 300°
pie crust	20-40 min.	400° - 500°

Vegetables & Fruits

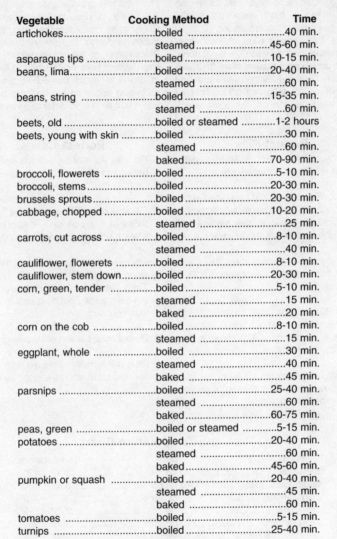

Vegetable	Cooking Method	Time
artichokes	boiled	40 min.
	steamed	45-60 min.
asparagus tips	boiled	10-15 min.
beans, lima	boiled	20-40 min.
	steamed	60 min.
beans, string	boiled	15-35 min.
	steamed	60 min.
beets, old	boiled or steamed	1-2 hours
beets, young with skin	boiled	30 min.
	steamed	60 min.
	baked	70-90 min.
broccoli, flowerets	boiled	5-10 min.
broccoli, stems	boiled	20-30 min.
brussels sprouts	boiled	20-30 min.
cabbage, chopped	boiled	10-20 min.
	steamed	25 min.
carrots, cut across	boiled	8-10 min.
	steamed	40 min.
cauliflower, flowerets	boiled	8-10 min.
cauliflower, stem down	boiled	20-30 min.
corn, green, tender	boiled	5-10 min.
	steamed	15 min.
	baked	20 min.
corn on the cob	boiled	8-10 min.
	steamed	15 min.
eggplant, whole	boiled	30 min.
	steamed	40 min.
	baked	45 min.
parsnips	boiled	25-40 min.
	steamed	60 min.
	baked	60-75 min.
peas, green	boiled or steamed	5-15 min.
potatoes	boiled	20-40 min.
	steamed	60 min.
	baked	45-60 min.
pumpkin or squash	boiled	20-40 min.
	steamed	45 min.
	baked	60 min.
tomatoes	boiled	5-15 min.
turnips	boiled	25-40 min.

Drying Time Table

Fruit	Sugar or Honey	Cooking Time
apricots	¼ c. for each cup of fruit	about 40 min.
figs	1 T. for each cup of fruit	about 30 min.
peaches	¼ c. for each cup of fruit	about 45 min.
prunes	2 T. for each cup of fruit	about 45 min.

Vegetables & Fruits

Buying Fresh Vegetables

Artichokes: Look for compact, tightly closed heads with green, clean-looking leaves. Avoid those with leaves that are brown or separated.

Asparagus: Stalks should be tender and firm; tips should be close and compact. Choose the stalks with very little white; they are more tender. Use asparagus soon because it toughens rapidly.

Beans, Snap: Those with small seeds inside the pods are best. Avoid beans with dry-looking pods.

Broccoli, Brussels Sprouts and Cauliflower: Flower clusters on broccoli and cauliflower should be tight and close together. Brussels sprouts should be firm and compact. Smudgy, dirty spots may indicate pests or disease.

Cabbage and Head Lettuce: Choose heads that are heavy for their size. Avoid cabbage with worm holes and lettuce with discoloration or soft rot.

Cucumbers: Choose long, slender cucumbers for best quality. May be dark or medium green, but yellow ones are undesirable.

Mushrooms: Caps should be closed around the stems. Avoid black or brown gills.

Peas and Lima Beans: Select pods that are well-filled but not bulging. Avoid dried, spotted, yellow, or flabby pods.

Buying Fresh Fruits

Bananas: Skin should be free of bruises and black or brown spots. Purchase them green and allow them to ripen at home at room temperature.

Berries: Select plump, solid berries with good color. Avoid stained containers which indicate wet or leaky berries. Berries with clinging caps, such as blackberries and raspberries, may be unripe. Strawberries without caps may be overripe.

Melons: In cantaloupes, thick, close netting on the rind indicates best quality. Cantaloupes are ripe when the stem scar is smooth and the space between the netting is yellow or yellow-green. They are best when fully ripe with fruity odor.

Honeydews are ripe when rind has creamy to yellowish color and velvety texture. Immature honeydews are whitish-green.

Ripe watermelons have some yellow color on one side. If melons are white or pale green on one side, they are not ripe.

Oranges, Grapefruit and Lemons: Choose those heavy for their size. Smoother, thinner skins usually indicate more juice. Most skin markings do not affect quality. Oranges with a slight greenish tinge may be just as ripe as fully colored ones. Light or greenish-yellow lemons are more tart than deep yellow ones. Avoid citrus fruits showing withered, sunken or soft areas.

Napkin Folding

General Tips:
Use well-starched linen napkins if possible. For more complicated folds, 24-inch napkins work best. Practice the folds with newspapers. Children can help. Once they learn the folds, they will have fun!

Shield

Easy fold. Elegant with monogram in corner.

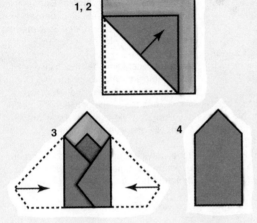

Instructions:
1. Fold into quarter size. If monogrammed, ornate corner should face down.
2. Turn up folded corner three-quarters.
3. Overlap right side and left side points.
4. Turn over; adjust sides so that they are even, single point in center.
5. Place point up or down on plate, or left of plate.

Rosette

Elegant on plate.

Instructions:
1. Fold left and right edges to center, leaving 1/2" opening along center.
2. Pleat firmly from top edge to bottom edge. Sharpen edges with hot iron.
3. Pinch center together. If necessary, use small piece of pipe cleaner to secure and top with single flower.
4. Spread out rosette.

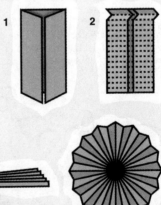

Napkin Folding

Candle

Easy to do; can be decorated.

Instructions:
1. Fold into triangle, point at top.
2. Turn lower edge up 1".
3. Turn over, folded edge down.
4. Roll tightly from left to right.
5. Tuck in corner. Stand upright.

Fan

Pretty in napkin ring or on plate.

Instructions:
1. Fold top and bottom edges to center.
2. Fold top and bottom edges to center a second time.
3. Pleat firmly from the left edge. Sharpen edges with hot iron.
4. Spread out fan. Balance flat folds of each side on table. Well-starched napkins will hold shape.

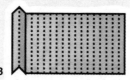

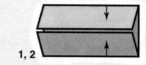

Lily

Effective and pretty on table.

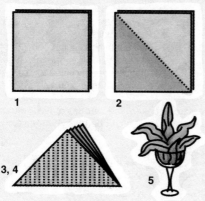

Instructions:
1. Fold napkin into quarters.
2. Fold into triangle, closed corner to open points.
3. Turn two points over to other side. (Two points are on either side of closed point.)
4. Pleat.
5. Place closed end in glass. Pull down two points on each side and shape.

Measurements
& Substitutions

Measurements

a pinch	1/8 teaspoon or less
3 teaspoons	1 tablespoon
4 tablespoons	1/4 cup
8 tablespoons	1/2 cup
12 tablespoons	3/4 cup
16 tablespoons	1 cup
2 cups	1 pint
4 cups	1 quart
4 quarts	1 gallon
8 quarts	1 peck
4 pecks	1 bushel
16 ounces	1 pound
32 ounces	1 quart
1 ounce liquid	2 tablespoons
8 ounces liquid	1 cup

**Use standard measuring spoons and cups.
All measurements are level.**

Substitutions

Ingredient	Quantity	Substitute
baking powder	1 teaspoon	1/4 tsp. baking soda plus 1/2 tsp. cream of tartar
catsup or chili sauce	1 cup	1 c. tomato sauce plus 1/2 c. sugar and 2 T. vinegar (for use in cooking)
chocolate	1 square (1 oz.)	3 or 4 T. cocoa plus 1 T. butter
cornstarch	1 tablespoon	2 T. flour or 2 tsp. quick-cooking tapioca
cracker crumbs	3/4 cup	1 c. bread crumbs
dates	1 lb.	1 1/2 c. dates, pitted and cut
dry mustard	1 teaspoon	1 T. prepared mustard
flour, self-rising	1 cup	1 c. all-purpose flour, 1/2 tsp. salt, and 1 tsp. baking powder
herbs, fresh	1 tablespoon	1 tsp. dried herbs
milk, sour	1 cup	1 T. lemon juice or vinegar plus sweet milk to make 1 c. (let stand 5 minutes)
whole	1 cup	1/2 c. evaporated milk plus 1/2 c. water
min. marshmallows	10	1 lg. marshmallow
onion, fresh	1 small	1 T. instant minced onion, rehydrated
sugar, brown	1/2 cup	2 T. molasses in 1/2 c. granulated sugar
powdered	1 cup	1 c. granulated sugar plus 1 tsp. cornstarch
tomato juice	1 cup	1/2 c. tomato sauce plus 1/2 c. water

**When substituting cocoa for chocolate in cakes, the amount of flour must
be reduced. Brown and white sugars usually can be interchanged.**

Equivalency Chart

Food	Quantity	Yield
apple	1 medium	1 cup
banana, mashed	1 medium	1/3 cup
bread	1 1/2 slices	1 cup soft crumbs
bread	1 slice	1/4 cup fine, dry crumbs
butter	1 stick or 1/4 pound	1/2 cup
cheese, American, cubed	1 pound	2 2/3 cups
American, grated	1 pound	5 cups
cream cheese	3-ounce package	6 2/3 tablespoons
chocolate, bitter	1 square	1 ounce
cocoa	1 pound	4 cups
coconut	1 1/2 pound package	2 2/3 cups
coffee, ground	1 pound	5 cups
cornmeal	1 pound	3 cups
cornstarch	1 pound	3 cups
crackers, graham	14 squares	1 cup fine crumbs
saltine	28 crackers	1 cup fine crumbs
egg	4-5 whole	1 cup
whites	8-10	1 cup
yolks	10-12	1 cup
evaporated milk	1 cup	3 cups whipped
flour, cake, sifted	1 pound	4 1/2 cups
rye	1 pound	5 cups
white, sifted	1 pound	4 cups
white, unsifted	1 pound	3 3/4 cups
gelatin, flavored	3 1/4 ounces	1/2 cup
unflavored	1/4 ounce	1 tablespoon
lemon	1 medium	3 tablespoon juice
marshmallows	16	1/4 pound
noodles, cooked	8-ounce package	7 cups
uncooked	4 ounces (1 1/2 cups)	2-3 cups cooked
macaroni, cooked	8-ounce package	6 cups
macaroni, uncooked	4 ounces (1 1/4 cups)	2 1/4 cups cooked
spaghetti, uncooked	7 ounces	4 cups cooked
nuts, chopped	1/4 pound	1 cup
almonds	1 pound	3 1/2 cups
walnuts, broken	1 pound	3 cups
walnuts, unshelled	1 pound	1 1/2 to 1 3/4 cups
onion	1 medium	1/2 cup
orange	3-4 medium	1 cup juice
raisins	1 pound	3 1/2 cups
rice, brown	1 cup	4 cups cooked
converted	1 cup	3 1/2 cups cooked
regular	1 cup	3 cups cooked
wild	1 cup	4 cups cooked
sugar, brown	1 pound	2 1/2 cups
powdered	1 pound	3 1/2 cups
white	1 pound	2 cups
vanilla wafers	22	1 cup fine crumbs
zwieback, crumbled	4	1 cups

Food Quantities
For Large Servings

	25 Servings	50 Servings	100 Servings
Beverages:			
coffee	½ pound and 1 ½ gallons water	1 pound and 3 gallons water	2 pounds and 6 gallons water
lemonade	10-15 lemons and 1 ½ gallons water	20-30 lemons and 3 gallons water	40-60 lemons and 6 gallons water
tea	¹/₁₂ pound and 1 ½ gallons water	⅙ pound and 3 gallons water	⅓ pound and 6 gallons water
Desserts:			
layered cake	1 12" cake	3 10" cakes	6 10" cakes
sheet cake	1 10" x 12" cake	1 12" x 20" cake	2 12" x 20" cakes
watermelon	37 ½ pounds	75 pounds	150 pounds
whipping cream	¾ pint	1 ½ to 2 pints	3-4 pints
Ice cream:			
brick	3 ¼ quarts	6 ½ quarts	13 quarts
bulk	2 ¼ quarts	4 ½ quarts or 1 ¼ gallons	9 quarts or 2 ½ gallons
Meat, poultry or fish:			
fish	13 pounds	25 pounds	50 pounds
fish, fillets or steak	7 ½ pounds	15 pounds	30 pounds
hamburger	9 pounds	18 pounds	35 pounds
turkey or chicken	13 pounds	25 to 35 pounds	50 to 75 pounds
wieners (beef)	6 ½ pounds	13 pounds	25 pounds
Salads, casseroles:			
baked beans	¾ gallon	1 ¼ gallons	2 ½ gallons
jello salad	¾ gallon	1 ¼ gallons	2 ½ gallons
potato salad	4 ¼ quarts	2 ¼ gallons	4 ½ gallons
scalloped potatoes	4 ½ quarts or 1 12" x 20" pan	9 quarts or 2 ¼ gallons	18 quarts 4 ½ gallons
spaghetti	1 ¼ gallons	2 ½ gallons	5 gallons
Sandwiches:			
bread	50 slices or 3 1-pound loaves	100 slices or 6 1-pound loaves	200 slices or 12 1-pound loaves
butter	½ pound	1 pound	2 pounds
lettuce	1 ½ heads	3 heads	6 heads
mayonnaise	1 cup	2 cups	4 cups
mixed filling			
meat, eggs, fish	1 ½ quarts	3 quarts	6 quarts
jam, jelly	1 quart	2 quarts	4 quarts

Microwave Hints

1. Place an open box of hardened brown sugar in the microwave oven with 1 cup hot water. Microwave on high for 1 1/2 to 2 minutes for 1/2 pound or 2 to 3 minutes for 1 pound.

2. Soften hard ice cream by microwaving at 30% power. One pint will take 15 to 30 seconds; one quart, 30-45 seconds; and one-half gallon, 45-60 seconds.

3. To melt chocolate, place 1/2 pound in glass bowl or measuring cup. Melt uncovered at 50% power for 3-4 minutes; stir after 2 minutes.

4. Soften one 8-ounce package of cream cheese by microwaving at 30% power for 2 to 2 1/2 minutes. One 3-ounce package of cream cheese will soften in 1 1/2 to 2 minutes.

5. A 4 1/2 ounce carton of whipped topping will thaw in 1 minute on the defrost setting. Whipped topping should be slightly firm in the center, but it will blend well when stirred. Do not over thaw!

6. Soften jello that has set up too hard - perhaps you were to chill it until slightly thickened and forgot it. Heat on a low power setting for a very short time.

7. Heat hot packs. A wet fingertip towel will take about 25 seconds. It depends on the temperature of the water used to wet the towel.

8. To scald milk, cook 1 cup for 2 to 2 1/2 minutes, stirring once each minute.

9. To make dry bread crumbs, cut 6 slices of bread into 1/2-inch cubes. Microwave in 3-quart casserole 6-7 minutes, or until dry, stirring after 3 minutes. Crush in blender.

10. Refresh stale potato chips, crackers or other snacks of such type by putting a plateful in the microwave for 30-45 seconds. Let stand for 1 minute to crisp. Cereals can also be crisped.

11. Nuts will be easier to shell if you place 2 cups of nuts in a 1-quart casserole with 1 cup of water. Cook for 4 to 5 minutes and the nutmeats will slip out whole after cracking the shell.

12. Stamp collectors can place a few drops of water on a stamp to remove it from an envelope. Heat in the microwave for 20 seconds, and the stamp will come off.

13. Using a round dish instead of a square one eliminates overcooked corners in baking cakes.

14. Sprinkle a layer of medium, finely chopped walnuts evenly onto the bottom and side of a ring pan or bundt cake pan to enhances the looks and eating quality. Pour in batter and microwave as recipe directs.

15. Do not salt foods on the surface as it causes dehydration and toughens food. Salt after you remove from the oven unless the recipe calls for using salt in the mixture.

16. Heat left-over custard and use it as frosting for a cake.

17. Melt marshmallow creme. Half of a 7-ounce jar will melt in 35-40 seconds on high. Stir to blend.

18. To toast coconut, spread 1/2 cup coconut in a pie plate and cook for 3-4 minutes, stirring every 30 seconds after 2 minutes. Watch closely, as it quickly browns.

19. To melt crystallized honey, heat uncovered jar on high for 30-45 seconds. If jar is large, repeat.

20. One stick of butter or margarine will soften in 1 minute when microwaved at 20% power.

Calorie Counter

Beverages

apple juice, 6 oz. 90
coffee (black) 0
cola type, 12 oz. 115
cranberry juice, 6 oz. 115
ginger ale, 12 oz. 115
grape juice, (prepared from
   frozen concentrate), 6 oz. 142
lemonade, (prepared from
   frozen concentrate), 6 oz. 85
milk, protein fortified, 1 c. 105
   skim, 1 c. 90
   whole, 1 c. 160
orange juice, 6 oz. 85
pineapple juice, unsweetened, 6 oz. 95
root beer, 12 oz. 150
tonic (quinine water) 12 oz. 132

Breads

cornbread, 1 sm. square 130
dumplings, 1 med. 70
French toast, 1 slice.........................135
melba toast, 1 slice 25
muffins, blueberry, 1 muffin 110
   bran, 1 muffin..............................106
   corn, 1 muffin 125
   English, 1 muffin 280
pancakes, 1 (4-in.) 60
pumpernickel, 1 slice 75
rye, 1 slice 60
waffle, 1 216
white, 1 slice 60-70
whole wheat, 1 slice 55-65

Cereals

cornflakes, 1 c. 105
cream of wheat, 1 c. 120
oatmeal, 1 c. 148
rice flakes, 1 c. 105
shredded wheat, 1 biscuit 100
sugar krisps, 3/4 c...........................110

Crackers

graham, 1 cracker.........................15-30
rye crisp, 1 cracker............................35
saltine, 1 cracker..........................17-20
wheat thins, 1 cracker 9

Dairy Products

butter or margarine, 1 T....................100
cheese, American, 1 oz.....................100
   camembert, 1 oz. 85
   cheddar, 1 oz................................115
   cottage cheese, 1 oz. 30
   mozzarella, 1 oz. 90
   parmesan, 1 oz. 130
   ricotta, 1 oz. 50
   roquefort, 1 oz. 105
   Swiss, 1 oz. 105
cream, light, 1 T. 30
   heavy, 1 T. 55
   sour, 1 T. 45
hot chocolate, with milk, 1 c. 277
milk chocolate, 1 oz. 145-155
yogurt
   made w/ whole milk, 1 c. 150-165
   made w/ skimmed milk, 1 c. 125

Eggs

fried, 1 lg. 100
poached or boiled, 1 lg. 75-80
scrambled or in omelet, 1 lg. 110-130

Fish and Seafood

bass, 4 oz. 105
salmon, broiled or baked, 3 oz. 155
sardines, canned in oil, 3 oz. 170
trout, fried, 3 1/2 oz. 220
tuna, in oil, 3 oz. 170
   in water, 3 oz. 110

Calorie Counter

Fruits

apple, 1 med. 80-100
applesauce, sweetened, 1/2 c. 90-115
   unsweetened, 1/2 c. 50
banana, 1 med. 85
blueberries, 1/2 c. 45
cantaloupe, 1/2 c. 24
cherries (pitted), raw, 1/2 c. 40
grapefruit, 1/2 med. 55
grapes, 1/2 c. 35-55
honeydew, 1/2 c. 55
mango, 1 med. 90
orange, 1 med. 65-75
peach, 1 med. 35
pear, 1 med. 60-100
pineapple, fresh, 1/2 c. 40
   canned in syrup, 1/2 c. 95
plum, 1 med. 30
strawberries, fresh, 1/2 c. 30
   frozen and sweetened, 1/2 c. 120-140
tangerine, 1 lg. 39
watermelon, 1/2 c. 42

Meat and Poultry

beef, ground (lean), 3 oz. 185
   roast, 3 oz. 185
chicken, broiled, 3 oz. 115
lamb chop (lean), 3 oz. 175-200
steak, sirloin, 3 oz. 175
   tenderloin, 3 oz. 174
   top round, 3 oz. 162
turkey, dark meat, 3 oz. 175
   white meat, 3 oz. 150
veal, cutlet, 3 oz. 156
   roast, 3 oz. 76

Nuts

almonds, 2 T. 105
cashews, 2 T. 100
peanuts, 2 T. 105
peanut butter, 1 T. 95
pecans, 2 T. 95
pistachios, 2 T. 92
walnuts, 2 T. 80

Pasta

macaroni or spaghetti,
   cooked, 3/4 c. 115

Salad Dressings

blue cheese, 1 T. 70
French, 1 T. 65
Italian, 1 T. 80
mayonnaise, 1 T. 100
olive oil, 1 T. 124
Russian, 1 T. 70
salad oil, 1 T. 120

Soups

bean, 1 c. 130-180
beef noodle, 1 c. 70
bouillon and consomme, 1 c. 30
chicken noodle, 1 c. 65
chicken with rice, 1 c. 50
minestrone, 1 c. 80-150
split pea, 1 c. 145-170
tomato with milk, 1 c. 170
vegetable, 1 c. 80-100

Vegetables

asparagus, 1 c. 35
broccoli, cooked, 1/2 c. 25
cabbage, cooked, 1/2 c. 15-20
carrots, cooked, 1/2 c. 25-30
cauliflower, 1/2 c. 10-15
corn (kernels), 1/2 c. 70
green beans, 1 c. 30
lettuce, shredded, 1/2 c. 5
mushrooms, canned, 1/2 c. 20
onions, cooked, 1/2 c. 30
peas, cooked, 1/2 c. 60
potato, baked, 1 med. 90
   chips, 8-10 100
   mashed, w/milk & butter, 1 c. ..200-300
spinach, 1 c. 40
tomato, raw, 1 med. 25
   cooked, 1/2 c. 30

Cooking Terms

Au gratin: Topped with crumbs and/or cheese and browned in oven or under broiler.

Au jus: Served in its own juices.

Baste: To moisten foods during cooking with pan drippings or special sauce in order to add flavor and prevent drying.

Bisque: A thick cream soup.

Blanch: To immerse in rapidly boiling water and allow to cook slightly.

Cream: To soften a fat, especially butter, by beating it at room temperature. Butter and sugar are often creamed together, making a smooth, soft paste.

Crimp: To seal the edges of a two-crust pie either by pinching them at intervals with the fingers or by pressing them together with the tines of a fork.

Crudites: An assortment of raw vegetables (i.e. carrots, broccoli, celery, mushrooms) that is served as an hors d'oeuvre, often accompanied by a dip.

Degrease: To remove fat from the surface of stews, soups, or stock. Usually cooled in the refrigerator so that fat hardens and is easily removed.

Dredge: To coat lightly with flour, cornmeal, etc.

Entree: The main course.

Fold: To incorporate a delicate substance, such as whipped cream or beaten egg whites, into another substance without releasing air bubbles. A spatula is used to gently bring part of the mixture from the bottom of the bowl to the top. The process is repeated, while slowly rotating the bowl, until the ingredients are thoroughly blended.

Glaze: To cover with a glossy coating, such as a melted and somewhat diluted jelly for fruit desserts.

Julienne: To cut vegetables, fruits, or cheeses into match-shaped slivers.

Marinate: To allow food to stand in a liquid in order to tenderize or to add flavor.

Meuniére: Dredged with flour and sautéed in butter.

Mince: To chop food into very small pieces.

Parboil: To boil until partially cooked; to blanch. Usually final cooking in a seasoned sauce follows this procedure.

Pare: To remove the outermost skin of a fruit or vegetable.

Poach: To cook gently in hot liquid kept just below the boiling point.

Purée: To mash foods by hand by rubbing through a sieve or food mill, or by whirling in a blender or food processor until perfectly smooth.

Refresh: To run cold water over food that has been parboiled in order to stop the cooking process quickly.

Sauté: To cook and/or brown food in a small quantity of hot shortening.

Scald: To heat to just below the boiling point, when tiny bubbles appear at the edge of the saucepan.

Simmer: To cook in liquid just below the boiling point. The surface of the liquid should be barely moving, broken from time to time by slowly rising bubbles.

Steep: To let food stand in hot liquid in order to extract or to enhance flavor, like tea in hot water or poached fruit in sugar syrup.

Toss: To combine ingredients with a repeated lifting motion.

Whip: To beat rapidly in order to incorporate air and produce expansion, as in heavy cream or egg whites.